Healing Through Spirit * Living In Love

Rev. Jenn Shepherd

Copyright © 2012 Rev. Jenn Shepherd

All rights reserved.

ISBN:1494746352
ISBN-13:9781494746353

DEDICATION

SPECIAL THANKS

I was told once that miracles happen in the tragedies and that my serving Spirit would be and is one of those miracles.

My husband, Dean, and I met when we were twelve. We were friends in school and remained in contact after the scattering that happens after school. He picked me up after my first marriage crumbled and we dated for many years before marrying in 2005. He became step-dad to my two boys and we added two more boys to the family in 2007 and 2008. We were comfortable, happy, full of expectations. Thanksgiving time of 2009 we took the family to Disney World. A beautiful experience. Soon after this trip Dean started to not feel well. In the spring time of 2010 Dean was hurting and by fall he had pneumonia and what appeared to be a ruptured disk. Long story short Dean and I spent Christmas 2010 sharing his hospital bed at the Cleveland Clinic and he was diagnosed with a non-smokers form of lung cancer.

I was already practicing QiGong and Reiki before Dean was diagnosed. At the time I was doing it all for me and my own personal knowledge and development. I never thought I would be furthering knowledge and using it to help him through such a time. The nurse that walked us though what to do for chemo treatments and managing the side effects strongly suggested we look into things like Reiki and QiGong. It was at that moment I decided that what I was learning and practicing was no longer a hobby. Once I decided I discovered that the 'sixth sense' I have always had took on a new dimension. No longer was I merely psychic I discovered I was a medium as well. This led Dean and I to find The First Spiritualist Church to not only help understand what was going on with me but also give us both a healing place while dealing with his cancer.

The healing knowledge and training coupled with a fuller understanding of how Spirit works in all our lives aided Dean, the family and myself through his time of illness and his passing Sept. 27, 2012. Dean did not need any type of narcotic pain medication until a couple of weeks before he transitioned and I know even though his body was not "cured" by what we were doing and the modalities we used his mind and spirit were healed and he was ready to transition when he did. Healing through Spirit allowed Dean and I to experience his passing together. Understanding how Spirit works has allowed me to know when he is sending love. My personal relationship with Spirit allows me to serve Spirit by helping others with healing on all levels.

Dean always encouraged my 'craziness'. He understood the energy work, the healing work and the connections I have with Spirit. He encouraged my ministry studies and allowed me to 'practice' on him repeatedly. It was through the experience I had with him in his transition that allowed me to see, know and feel Spirit in a way I am not sure would have been possible for me without that experience. His story is a part of mine. He continues to encourage. For that and his love I will ever be grateful.

CONTENTS

1. INTRODUCTION — PG #1
2. LIGHT — PG #5
3. CHOICES FOR TODAY — PG #7
4. ARE THERE ANGELS? — PG #12
5. LOVE AND LIFE — PG #16
6. TRAVELING THE NIGHT — PG #21
7. ASSESSING THE LIGHT — PG #23
8. FORWARD — PG #26
9. CHERRYBLOSSOMS — PG #30
10. RAINBOW CONNECTION — PG #32
11. LANGUAGE — PG #35
12. GRATITUDE — PG #42
13. PRAYING — PG #46
14. HEALING — PG #49
15. CHARLIE — PG #62
16. POURING LOVE — PG #66
17. MYSTICS DREAM — PG #70
18. SILENCE — PG #73
19. FAERIES IN THE GARDEN — PG #77
20. WE ARE ALL CONNECTED — PG #80
21. WE ARE ALL ABLE TO FLY — PG #90
22. CONNECTING TO SPIRIT — PG #91
23. MEANING OF THE SEASON — PG #101
24. LOVE NEVER DIES — PG #105
25. COMPASSION — PG #115
26. STARBRIDGE — PG #120

ACKNOWLEDGMENTS

Special thanks to my children Michael, Lloyd, Galen and Cian. They are my daily grounding and inspiration.

Much gratitude to my parents: Janet and Don who have stood by me and offered unconditional love through every step of my journey.

Thank you to my siblings. Even though we do not always see a lot of each other there is a connection that transcends and the positive thoughts and love are always appreciated.

Much love to Karen and Erin who have listened, encouraged and offer seemingly endless support.

Appreciation extended to my development circle. This is the group that allowed for expression and practice and an incredible amount of self-confidence.

Special thanks to Natalie who not only leads the development circle but also was instrumental in my ministry studies.

Heartfelt love and blessings for Jake, who without I may never have compiled these writings. His enthusiasm, trust and often times strikingly different viewpoints than my own have allowed me to find ways to express my relationship with Spirit and to enhance the gifts I have to serve Spirit with in ways that I did not trust I was capable before he entered my life. For this and much more he has my love and my gratitude.

Rev. Jenn Shepherd

1 INTRODUCTION

As hard as I have tried in this writing endeavor to find one topic and then just write, it has been mostly impossible to not allow my fingers and mind to write what is available at the time.

During the last 3 years I have been able to take what is available in the way of inspiration throughout the day and what is going on with my own personal inner spiritual path and struggle to write a blog.

That blog is in many ways a complete manifestation out of the need for some type of outlet during the time my husband was diagnosed, suffered through and passed because of cancer. It was a very healthy way for me to allow people that were concerned for our family to know what was going on with us and also to allow Spirit to remind me that I was not alone at all during those days.

I wanted a way to express what I have learned and what I am still learning and what I am teaching in classes each and every week in this book. There is already another book which is a compilation of the blog entries expressing in detail the journey through sickness and passing. I wanted to somehow get away from that story. Eckhart Tolle says that we all have stories; it does not mean we ARE the stories. I totally believe that.

I have come to realize, however, that each and every "story" in my life has availed a way in which I am able to grow and develop and understand. I may not BE my story, but in a lot of ways who I am today and what I am able to understand is the direct product of those stories.

Cancer is only one of my stories. That is the one, however that was not hidden. That has also been a lesson for me.

I was married at the age of 21. That marriage blessed me with two sons. It also was a time in which I had to learn how to stick up for myself as a person. I still do not talk much about that story, because of my children and a need on my part either correct or not to still protect them from that story.

There are other stories along the way. There are stories of grieving over grandparents passing, a cousin taking herself to Spirit, children with learning disabilities, being a single mother, remarrying while working for a parochial school, friends coming and going, depression during and after pregnancies, financial issues, a husband diagnosed with terminal cancer leaving me with two little ones to care for in an all too familiar single parent home and the learning and struggle that came when healing, mediumship and ministry became my life. The learning that is still taking place on how to handle myself, balancing the responsibility between my family and children and serving and growing in Spirit. Finding the balance between the people that will encourage and support and the people who will judge and become negative is another part of the story.

Those lessons, those times, those memories will ALWAYS be with each and every one of us. It does not matter how many pages in a book the story may entail. It does not matter how many people know or were involved in that part of your story. The story will always be remembered in a way that you perceived it. The story will always be a place to understand where you had choices to make and how you either grew or did not grow through the experience. They are bench marks not of success or failure but of times in your life where change was evident.

The change I want to leave behind is the "cancer story". This will not happen as soon as I may like. I have small children who still struggle with the loss of a dad. I still find myself melancholy on some days, especially holidays and need to remind myself that it is alright to remember in the midst of writing new pages in my life story. It is possible to remember and learn without BECOMING the story.

That all being said. I have decided not to fight the process that has been evolving here in these pages. Some are anecdotal and some are not. Some are more poetic and some are taken directly from parts of the blog that has been already written. I am finding that through the writing the main theme is to find your own unique pathway with Divine. Your walk, your path, your stories and lessons from the stories are going to be different than mine. They are going to be different than anyone else's on this planet. The path is one that is most needed for you to learn what you need to learn so that when you return HOME you will be that much closer to understanding the love from which we are all created.

Unfortunately we are not able to understand what we have available to us until it seems so totally absent from our life. We need to learn to cultivate love and find it in the most drastic times in order to understand that it is there to draw on at any time.

We need to sometimes feel out of complete control of our own story to understand that all we need to do is stand up, grab the pen and start writing the story we would like. The details of the story may always get a little blurred, but this allows for an adjustment once again, a choice and a learning experience. We are here to learn what love is and to help others realize it themselves. If we accomplish this task with ourselves and just one other soul on the planet then our mission here has been successful and we will be one step closer to the Source of Light.

2 LIGHT

The sky is filled with energy and light.
Stretching to the Universe and the Cosmos there is a bridge.
The bridge of light and truth;
The bridge we are allowed to walk in times of turmoil and strife;
The lighted was to our past, present and future.

Hold onto the Light as we travel.
Travelers of every size, shape and color,
Travelers we know and love,
Travelers new and inviting.

Familiarity...
Embrace...
Divine connections drawing us Home.

Answers dwell in the Light of the Stars.
Energy of truth radiates color through the Universe
Scenes of tranquility;
Touches of Fate;
The embrace of the old ways all while being grounded in the now.

Life's lessons growing.
Details clear.
Traveling the Light bridge;
Holding Hands,
Not letting go,
Forever together.

Connected...
Learning...
Spirit Shining Bright.

Soaring...
Giving...
Feeling ...
Breathing...
Knowing...

Holding out our hands we understand.
Allowing Light to support the walk we grow.
Allowing knowledge and trust we are.

And so it is.

3 CHOICES FOR TODAY

(July 2013)
This weekend I had some choices to make.

This past Saturday, the 27th, marked 10 months since Dean crossed over into Spirit.

This past Saturday was also a time in which many former classmates arrived into town in celebration of 25 years of life after high school. There were people I wanted to see ... honestly since Dean and I graduated the same class I was having trouble wrapping my brain around seeing them alone.

This weekend I chose to attend a Master Peng QiGong workshop developing in meditation and learning a new practice set, spend the evenings/overnight at Lily Dale and being with a few new friends. Something for ME.

While I was away there seemed to be a theme to the weekend. In fact... at one point, in the dark, during a rain I decided to puddle splash while others looked on and smiled, Tim Brainard stopped and asked what I was doing in the rain. My friend Erin had found a little dining tent put up with a couple of picnic tables under it and Tim sat with us a while and told us stories. Stories solidifying the weekend's theme of BE YOURSELF.

"Say who you are." "BE YOU!"

Knowing that are no coincidences I have taken what Tim stopped to share to heart. I really thought I had been doing a pretty good of being myself lately. In fact, another friend of mine expressed to me not to long ago that this is something that I have taught her in the past few months. She relayed a story about how things in the house and with people around me and situations seemed to be totally out of control fairly soon after Dean had passed. I do not remember the whole discussion with her at that time. She recalls that the topic came up as to what I was going to do to take care of all those things, issues and situations. She said that I told her those things were not up to me .. that I did not need to fix them since most were other people's issues. I guess I was a bit of a potty mouth about it and told her that I did not give a fuck what other people thought since in the grand scheme of things it really did not matter. I told her it only mattered that I was comfortable and my children were adjusting. She said she took that to heart and made adjustments in her own life that has allowed stress to minimize in her life.

I am glad she told me that story. It has made me try even harder to remember to just be me, since in that instance it helped someone else.

Sometimes it is admittedly hard as we each seem to be in a sea of labels:
Widow
Mother
Daughter
Teacher
Friend
Healer
Minister
Secretary
Medium
Photographer
Alumni

We all have labels.

Labels are a reality of the human condition. Labels are restrictive because of the inadequacies of human language.

We are LOVE.

We are expressions of Divine; each of us a bit of a different expression ... on the road to knowledge and realization of that Love that has been placed in each and every one of us at the very moment of creation.

Realizing that ... knowing that our uniqueness is what helps spur the learning and knowledge for all of us seeking Universal development and unity with the Divine that connects us all... .. How can any of us even try to be anything that we are not meant to be?

There are no obstacles for trueness. What one needs will be there. The opportunities, the people, the situations, and eventually the realization that in the total UNDERSTANDING that when we are who we really are and NOT try and fit into any kind of mold ... UNDERSTAND that we will have not only what we WANT but what we NEED for everything when we KNOW that all is possible.

Faith of a MUSTARD SEED.

NOT

Belief of a MUSTARD SEED.

Faith is a KNOWING,
Belief is an OPINION.

I KNOW that I will be able to support my family through Healing work and teaching and Ministry work and teaching is TOTALLY different than if I would say "maybe" or "believe".

I KNOW I am more than the labels; especially the "widow" label. Some of the labels I am fond of, really ... but none of them really, really express who I am. Only I know, really if I am staying true to that and the path that I have developed with **Divine Spirit.**

When talking and interacting with others I realize that only they know as well. Why judgment is no ridiculous. Realizing the LOVE and the DIVINE spark that each of us has will allow interaction without judgment, without prejudice and with a love for all.

Finding who we really are and who we really want to be may take some time, meditation and prayer.

The trick is -- NOW. Taking JUST TODAY and being you.
JUST TODAY taking time to practice and train.
JUST TODAY meditating.
JUST TODAY remembering to LOVE.
JUST TODAY choose to be HAPPY.
JUST TODAY being PRESENT.
JUST TODAY ..... the Universe really does not understand Tomorrow or Yesterday.

4 ARE THERE ANGELS?

I purchased Christmas cards for Christmas 2012 with a beautiful depiction of the angel Uriel. If one uses the Roman Catholic Calendar he has a 'feast day' of September 29th. This is my son Lloyd's birthday. This means from a Roman Catholic stand point Uriel becomes one of Lloyd's 'patron saints'. Patron saints are said to be the ones that a person can go to in times of help and pray to them when needed. Other religions, including Spiritualists, hold that there are guides to help us. In this way the notion that there is a patron or a guardian angel for each of us is about the same thing, but set in a different set of vocabulary and dogma.

In September of 2012 Dean and I visited the doctor one more time. In that visit Dean learned that some of his recent efforts at curing the cancer did not work. He learned that the place he had gone to for treatment either was terribly unreliable in their approach or incredibly unethical or a little of both since they told him that his cancer was receding and in fact it had grown while he was away in Mexico for treatment. Dean decided that day to return home and involve hospice. I remember the doctor standing in front of both of us and trying to explain how it was important to make the best of whatever time was going to be available, that he respected Dean's decision and understood that it was the best for him.

I struggled the entire day. I was struggling while the doctor was speaking. Somewhere in the middle of his little speech on acceptance I was aware of a presence in the room. For me the presence made itself known behind the doctor. There was suddenly an overwhelming feeling of peace and understanding in the process that both Dean and I were going through at that very moment. Everything in my body until that point was screaming inside for Dean to just go back to the hospital one more time. Within that presence I understood the futility of any such efforts and how that really would do more harm for Dean than good. I realized that we were not alone. For me the vision of an angel coupled with the feeling of understanding and peace is what did the trick. I remember saying something to the doctor about how every good doctor must have an angel to help him, for it was much more my identification with the feelings being conveyed to me from Spirit that lent itself to acceptance than anything the doctor was trying to say.

I was so taken by what I felt and saw that I did a little search on the internet when I got home with Dean that evening. I found the photo I had created into cards right away. It had in the drawing everything I had been seeing over and over again the two weeks prior (the butterflies, the sunflowers, the incredibly vivid sunsets and bright stars. It also had the gold laced wings I had seen with the feelings of peace.) I looked up the name of the angel depiction and found it to be Uriel. I discovered he is associated with wisdom and truth; especially in trying situations. Everything I needed at that time, and in that place.

I had a friend say to me that angels are not real. He said that they are a manifestation of people's imaginations. Perhaps. It is possible that Divine responded to my internal struggle with what I would identify with to allow me to know that strength and love through spirit was still available to me and to my family through that situation. It is possible I saw what I needed to see. It is also possible that beings of Light take on all forms. It is possible that there are things in this grand Universe that we are just not privy to understand at this time and it will take returning Home to Spirit to be able to piece it all together. There are so many things way more powerful than us. There are energies and love that come together to comfort, heal, guide and help us maintain a relationship with the Creator in ways that best meet the needs and experiences of both our humanness and soul.

Take the time to realize when Spirit is touching in with you. There are signs every day. There are special songs on the radio, hugs, smiles, and shapes of snowflakes, laughter in children, seeing a special bird, or catching a certain phrase on the television. Any recognition is valid, if it touches you and brings you closer to Divine Love.

I saw an angel. I felt the peace associated with the seeing. It brought me closer to understanding the healing, forgiveness, support and complete and total love that is available when we allow ourselves to allow Divine to work with us and through us. It is possible someday I will understand my experience that day differently, but the effect will still be the same. As will any time I recognize and acknowledge Spirit's presence.

5 LOVE AND LIFE

In the realms of existence our consciousness desires growth and understanding.

The Divine Spark that created the Universe allows for creation to grow and develop. We, as the human component of creation were given one more gift: FREE WILL.

With this gift, this free will we may choose to understand the dichotomies of Light and Dark; Good and Evil. We may choose to strive for understanding with the Divine that created with Love. We may choose to merge with that Love and to share that Love.

In order to merge and share there needs to be an understanding. To understand something that is so innate in all creation it is necessary to learn what it is like WITHOUT such love. It is necessary to come to this solid state, a slower vibration of energy that we call matter. We need to become a fleshy human. We need to adorn the mask of "life". We put on our mask and join the masquerade party here on Earth and learn all the dances and routines necessary to understand how to choose and receive love. We stumble while we learn for it is very hard to see properly from inside our masks. We learn ways of coping, strategies that help us remember where we really came from and how to maintain the Light of our true existence and heritage in such a clumsy atmosphere.

We are not left completely alone in this masquerade. We are sent love. We are given guidance in the form of intuition, angles, and guides. There are those among us that have retained a sacred connection and become our grand seers and teachers. We read and learn from mystics living and past, saints, and those whose teachings excite such a vigor that whole religious structures were creates in their name. Buddha, Jesus and Muhammad are such as these.

There are many of us that flock to religion as a way to understand how the universe plays out in each and every one of us. We ask to know who we have a feeling of something greater. We want a barometer reading for our wants, desires and intuition. We look to the structures that have been built around philosophy and religion for stability thinking if we do the correct rituals, complete the correct prayers, wear the correct jewelry and clothing, if we claim that we are the follower of one particular name of God over another then we will be saved and be able to live forever in the Love of Creation.

The truth is that it doesn't matter the vocabulary set we use.

Yahweh	God	Divine	Christ
Universe	Allah	Spirit	One
Great Spirit	The Force Energy		Light

The bottom line is that we are all from Love.

The punitiveness of the religious structure that pervades rational intelligence and natural intuition and tries to create a state of fear by soaking the truth of abundant love in uncertainty and the possibility of a fiery servitude is absurd at best. This masquerade ball called Life on this planet Earth is all the trial we are ever going to need. This time of fleshy existence is the time we are absent of the absolute Love we were created and the Light available from Creation.

The eye opener for many is that we CHOOSE to be here. We choose to leave the existence filled with unending energetic love of Divine in order to learn how to love ourselves as Spirit loves us.

Earth is a laboratory. We experiment on how to make decisions, how to have compassion and light for each other without losing self. We learn how to boost each other on the way to understanding and not get in each other's unique pathway of discovery. In every laboratory there are some "failed" experiments. There are experiments that do not go the way that was hypothesized. In those moments we have true learning. We learn what part of the experiment did not work, we learn what variables need to be changed in the future. We learn how to forgive the error judgment or the lack of research that took place to form the original hypothesis.

Also, like every laboratory there are scientists of varying degrees of schooling and experience. Some come that are brand new on the scene. They have not seen a laboratory before and everything is new and shiny. It is very hard for some of the new apprentices to remember what is on the outside of the laboratory doors once coming in and being absorbed some completely in the new atmosphere. There are scientists that have been there a time or two. They try and help the newly arrived while still continuing to learn new techniques themselves.

The laboratory has everything and anything in terms of issues and problems to be solved. There are experiments on relationships, poverty, illness, servitude, war, politics, finances, friendships, nature, religions, technology, spirituality, understanding, ego, knowledge, survival, wealth, abundance, governments, school, careers, callings, addiction, sex, marriage, receiving and giving and many, many more.

Luckily for us there are windows surrounding the entire laboratory. The rest of the energetic Universe has access to the struggles going on within. Each of the workers and scientists came originally with the knowledge that there was much more than the experiments set before them. Each of the workers knew of the love which created them and the laboratory before entry. The choice to become so absorbed in the activity around them clouded that memory. There were a few that retained the knowledge and others that remembered that they had been given this gift after some of their experiments went so terribly wrong that a total readjustment of self was in order before another experiment could even begin. It was in that total feeling of nothingness and failure that the Light was able to shine once more allowing them to use their previous knowledge of Love to redirect future experiments and changing the foundation of all further hypotheses.

The windows that surround the facility bring in all the Light necessary to learn, improve, and grow and to know that they are not alone. The Light serves as a gentle reminder that their knowledge will travel with them when they emerge from their work.

6 TRAVELING THE NIGHT

It is dark. The dark road seems very, very long to travel. There are "things" in the shadows. There is trepidation. There is fear. There is .... moon light. Streaks of silver bouncing off the gray of the night shadow. Streaks of brightness, pure light trying, desperately to peak though the forbidden black to aid in the quest of the path. Sparkles of hope sprinkled with wonder and delight. To find more it is necessary to follow. It is necessary to come out from the underbrush and find the streaming that has made the sparkle. Find the beam that has made the streaming. Find the Brightness that has been reflected by the moon --- the pure source of light.

It is necessary sometimes to travel the entire night, chopping, cutting, getting scraped and gnarled by the unseen. But it is the perseverance that prevails. It is the perseverance that will allow the path to come into full view. The path littered with flowers instead of thorns. The path in which the moonlight has revealed the source of the sun. The path in which clouds may appear, but always float on by with the indifference of the traveler that knows that this IS THE correct path.

The trick is .. well, the want. Is there a want to understand where the sparkles come from. Is there even an inkling that we are looking for the sparkles that lead to the path, that lead to the source? If one is not looking, one will never find.

Peace of mind, a clearing, a wanting -- and then a follow-through.

Perhaps a rainbow appears while walking the path, the manifestation of all parts of the white light of the source. Beautiful, bright, always follows on the footsteps of the cloud. A wonderful reminder that there are many avenues, feelings, adventures yet on this path. That the White light is full of the radiance of all, manifesting in all colors, in all places, and shines more fully all these colors when it rains. The perpetual reminder that if one has found the path and stays true, everything will be all right at the end of the travels. Peace, security, happiness, wonderment and delight.

7 ASSESSING THE LIGHT

Each and every situation in our life, much like scientists setting up an experiment, is set up by us. There certainly are some variables that are not all our own doing, but what we do with those variables once presented and how we react with and towards them is all our own doing. The choices we make because of adversity in our lives help to shape who we are, and who we will become. It will shape the type of adversity we will see and encounter in our futures.

My own life is no different than many others. The names of my struggles may be different than another's but struggle I do to keep a balance. I struggle to remember the Light is always there. Spirit guides. We NEED to listen in order to have 'experiments' that have conclusions that allow us to emerge with a bit more understanding of how Love works in this

Universe. One more steps closer to merging with that Love for all eternity.

How do we listen? What do we need to do in order to listen and understand? What help is there for us to learn, grow and understand? Is it necessary for our experiments to go completely out of control and we feel like we are in complete darkness before we receive and understand the inspiration that is there? How does Spirit stay in touch with us while we are here? How do we know that we have not been left totally alone by choosing to learn and to dance on this Earth Masquerade Ball? How is it possible for us once reaching the despair of a shattered experiment to regroup and start again with a brand new hypothesis? What is our reward for doing just that? What is the incentive? How do we prevent more shattered experiments?

The simple answer is to take the time to listen and then to discern what we are hearing. There are many I know that tell me that they do exactly what they understand their guides want them to do all the time. In the just doing there is no discerning and there is no growth in the doing. When there is a conscious efforts on our part to not only listen but to also have a discourse with ourselves on the merit of such an action in our lives we grow in understanding. We also take ownership of our acting or not reacting. We take responsibility on how our lives are playing out and how we react in to the internal and external stimuli in our lives. We need to remember that we are indeed responsible. It is our personal responsibility to grow or not grow, to love or not to love, to learn or not to learn. To change the unique variables in the experiment of 'life' or to just allow the experiment to unfold around us is always OUR responsibility.

We ask for counsel. We attune ourselves more and more so that we understand the connections, we receive the guidance through intuition and sensitivities, we receive messages and knowings from loved ones, helpers and guides. Then WE make the appropriate action and decision. The outcomes of our unique experiment are never the fault of Spirit or the exact wish of Spirit. In fact we are the largest changing variable in our experiment. When we realize implicitly that the constant is Spirit's unconditional Love and our willingness or unwillingness to act with that love as an anchor is the greatest guide in how we deal with and cope with the struggles a human existence contains we realize that there really is no experiment to shatter. There is only the chance to learn to dance.

8 FORWARD

Ever think that the Universe if trying to bang you over the head with a lesson?

A recent lecture at church was all about moving forward. It was about not letting things in the past get in the way of your happiness now. It was about choosing to be happy, no matter what the circumstances. It was about our ability to create our own world despite whatever has happened to us in the past and whatever we have blamed our circumstances at present.

Last night my tea bag spoke to me in a way that it usually does not. I posted that photo along with a few thoughts onto Facebook. Since it is a reoccurring theme, that post and photo are below.

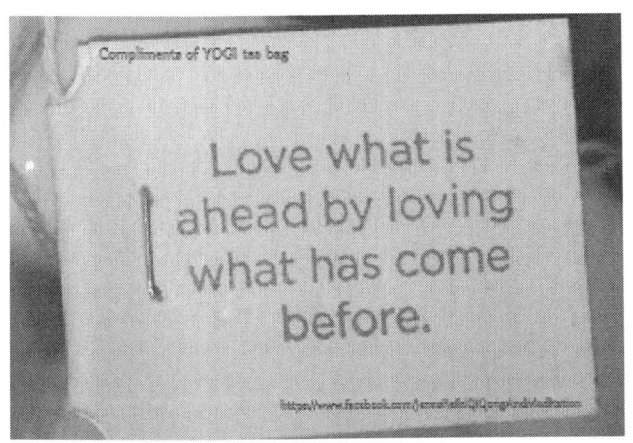

> Compliments of YOGI tea bag
>
> Love what is ahead by loving what has come before.

It is impossible for us to forget the past. What is possible is for us to learn from what has come before. Cherish Every Moment whether is, was "good" or "bad". ALL of those moments helped to create the person you are portraying today. Take some time to send LOVE to what has come before. Accept, Forgive, and Embrace...EVERYTHING. Then LOVE who you are now. LOVE what will be revealed to you as you walk into the future.

There is no way we could make the walk forward without tripping, stumbling, walking, laughing, dancing, skipping, daydreaming, strolling, racing and crawling the pathway that has come before.

BREATHE. LOVE. LAUGH. LIVE. SMILE and REJOICE that we have the ability to CHOOSE what comes ahead. Choices made from the wisdom of the walk already traveled.

The next two readings I did for people after I posted this

message were individuals making decisions about their future and their path and both were in some way very connected to what happened before and the memories of what happened before and the unwillingness to have some of the same set of occurrences happen as they did before. There is a reluctance to come out of the protective bubble that one is in to experience something new and different. There is a reluctance to get hurt or to hurt other people.

Thing is, other people have a choice just as we do. Other people CHOOSE to feel hurt. Other people CHOOSE to share in our experiences or decide that we are not the right person to be experiencing life. We CHOOSE if we are going to allow others to hurt us or accept who they are and where they are at. We choose if it is in our best interest for the path that is set before us to be around certain people and situations.

I think this is the hardest part. I know through changes in my life whole friendship groups disappeared. I also know that I have been incredibly fortunate in that some of those long time friends have reappeared, as it seems that our paths only needed to diverge for a short time for individual learning before coming back together again. No matter what happens, it does not mean that we cannot still extend love to those people that come in and out of our lives. We need to remember that we are responsible for OUR OWN actions ... not others. We need to understand that even if we did not do the best BEFORE and even if those around us did not do their best BEFORE the road only moves forward.

Sometimes it is pretty hard for me to not think about the past few years and not be completely pissed off *(I tried to find another less offensive word for here -- but, really, it is the one that fits)* at how my life has turned out. I mean, really... two marriages: one ending in divorce and the other ending because of the loveliness known as cancer, four children that all need support and attention and me seemingly going it alone **once again**. The road behind me filled with all kinds of heartache and tears, but also wonderful lessons, and also some very wonderful people.

I have a thank you list that I go down each and every night. I actually keep it tucked under a pillow so as I lie down I remember to be thankful, even if I have not taken the time yet that day. There are special people on that list; there are things like my car, and money and the clients and students. There is family, and the gifts that Spirit has given. There are seemingly silly things like my camera, computer and cell phone (which has not only helped my business grow but also has kept me in touch with some very special people). There is my church family and my Spirit Circle family. There are things added each night depending on what happened during the day. Remaining thankful and sending that thanks right to Divine has really, really helped me focus on what is important. Focus on NOW. It has helped greatly in my CHOOSING to be happy despite obstacles, trials, lessons and heartache.

It has helped me greatly look forward with a tremendous amount of HOPE.

9 CHERRY BLOSSOMS

The Spirit walks.

The Spirit Guides.

Always there is truth - there is nothing to hide.

Clear the way for never ending power. The power of knowledge. The power of Light. The power of closeness in the night.

We are the beloved, created of and by the Divine.

We live our lives here, to learn, to shine.

Caring, sharing - loving and living. Knowing that in the giving we are learning and receiving.

Cherry Blossoms fill the air in early spring - and yet the fruit takes months of growing in the sun. Becoming ripe with the goodness soaked up in the summer months.

There is power in that cherry tree to keep blooming year after year. It never gives up -- never stops producing fruit for other to pick, to share. To give back to nature. To make sweet jams, and pies. It blooms again and again, giving and giving just so others may enjoy. Stoic while naked in the winter, barren and seemingly without life. Yet, there is always life within. Pulsing in the roots below. Waiting for the right moment in which to bloom for all to see. Knowing that it is way too much effort to be in full bloom all the time. There does indeed need some time for rest. There needs to be some time to recharge. To meditate. To just be, listen, wait and know that the Divine Universe has a plan that will continue to unfold allowing it to shine, to bloom, to create and to give, to serve Spirit when the time is right.

10 RAINBOW CONNECTION

(It is highly recommended that one looks up the original Kermit Rainbow Connection on YouTube before and/or after reading this section)

"The lovers, the dreamers and me....

All of us under its spell -- we know that it's probably magic ...

Have you been half asleep -- and have you heard voices -- I've heard them calling my name. "

Rainbows are these incredible unique wonders of nature that come about because of the way our eyes perceive frequencies of light refracted with the proper measurement of both sunlight and water molecules.

Basically and "illusion" come to life -- not hidden in any fashion - flashing across the sky in beautiful colorful wonder when sun and rain meet.

Sun and rain -- opposites and yet both needed to create life as we know it. Both refreshing and cleansing at different times and in different ways. Washing or burning away the old, shining and creating a sparkling new.

Both ... opposites.. when mixed, when enjoyed, when noticed, when allowed to work together create such a wonder that people will stop exactly what they are doing to watch, comment on, and even chase the rainbow.

"Someone thought of that and someone believed it.
Look what it's done so far.
What's so amazing that keeps us stargazing and what do we think we might see?"

Allowing our thoughts to become reality. Allowing true expression of ourselves. Taking what the world gives us and mixing it with the Divine that is within ... looking up at the stars and knowing that there is so much more -- knowing that, we are part of something so much greater than ourselves.

Someday we will find that connection. The connection that the rainbow so readily shows when it mixes the best of rain, and sun and our own unique biological ability to see. Once we recognize that all parts can help complete the whole. That knowledge is everywhere .. that we ourselves are capable of being the lover and the dreamer while still being "me" what a completely beautiful and wonderful place this world can and will be.

"Somebody thought of it and someone believed it. Look what

its done so far"

Taking the time to spread the goodness, the gift of loving, the gift of dreaming, the gift of allowing many colors to shine for all to see -- look what good we will have.

It only takes one raindrop and one tiny ray of light to start a rainbow. It only takes one tiny little though followed by one tiny little voice of praise and well wishes, one tiny little prayer of healing and well-being, one tiny little action -- a "hello, how are you doing today" to brighten and extend the rainbow for more to see.

"Someday we will find it -- the rainbow connection - the lovers, the dreamers and me."

    Thank you Kermit.
Disclaimer (I do not suggest to hold any rights AT ALL to Kermit .. He and this song merely inspires).

11 LANGUAGE

Language is an interesting thing. It is beautiful in that it gives a vehicle for personal expression. It allows humans to be able to share thoughts and feelings. It allows for the transference of knowledge on a grand scale in both the verbal and written form. It also is cumbersome in a world in which there are so many different types of cultures, backgrounds, and indeed languages. Not only are there languages there are different dialects of the languages, there are different upbringings with each of the languages and there are dictionaries upon dictionaries that attempt to explain the meanings of words that have synonyms upon synonyms. In this realm of an imperfect communication system it is not so really hard to understand why it is so difficult sometimes to express oneself in a way that the majority of people will not only understand but understand without bias or judgment based on the vocabulary expressed.

Our religious system is one such quandary of language inadequacies. There are thousands of religions and within those religious sects or spinoffs all over the world. There are also different churches, communities and organizations all trying to get across and create an understanding of a particular belief system. There are many that are completely ancient, springing forth from a time when humans communed in a completely coexisting way with the natural world. There was a lot more 'feeling' in these methods of understanding where the human relationship is in the universe. There have sprung many great teachers in many different parts of the world. Some of these teachers were more science based or analytical in their approach to understanding the world. Many of them such as Plato and Aristotle have become philosophical icons and in their time laid the ground work for others to discover on their own the nature of human existence. There are other great teachers such as Buddha, Confucius, Jesus, and Muhammad who all have expressed an inner knowing about the nature of man. They have all expressed the idea in one form or another that indeed we are all one under one universal constant of love and that it is necessary to recognize this universal love in each other.

The nature of man is to take great teachings and organize in some fashion. The nature of some men is to use the brain too much and not rely on the feelings that are an innate gift in each and every one of us. Soon those who think drew up books and a set of rules. Soon there were rituals and certain ways of expressing that one understood one or the other teaching and made it his own. Soon there were quibbles about which words were the best and which traditions the best and which ceremonies the best in order to attain enlightenment.

In many ways humans have lost their ability to understand the true meaning in all of the words. We need words for the knowledge. We need words so that we are able to express to each other the FEELINGS and KNOWINGS that are possible in the complete silence of non-words. That in itself is a huge hurdle to overcome.

I have a predisposition for using the word Divine or Spirit when I talk about the great Universal constant of Creation. My inclination is to speak in terms of a Divine Intelligence that allows for expression of itself in life. My neighbor may be more comfortable with the term God and my friend may be more comfortable in speaking in terms of Energy. It is in the understanding that language is ONLY language and that we are each in our own unique way walking the path to enlightenment that will allow for the cessation for the amount of bickering and negative expression that is so prevalent in the world around us and shown though the expression of the evening and world news.

The recognition that each and every person on the planet has the ability and even the right to express their world in the vocabulary most comfortable for them and also express their reality in the most comfortable rituals and culture which is available to them would allow for a very unique discourse and end the need to endless bickering that occurs.

We are always going to find those people that speak our version of the language to bond with and create community. It is in these instances that structured communities such as churches are formed. These organizations become a detriment to themselves when the organization becomes more important than the souls brought together under the roof of the organization. Once the organization itself believes that it has the cornerstone on the correct vocabulary the growth and understanding of the community is stifled. It is the responsibility of the members within the community to be aware that they each have their own ability to grow and understand. It is the responsibility for each and every individual to create his own reality with Spirit and Divine. No organization, no matter how incredibly worthy, has the right to impede on an individual's growth and deepening relationship with the Love which created all.

The vocabulary in labeling oneself and organization is also a troubling proposition. Accepting the axiom that it is human nature to band together with like-minded individuals is also to accept the nature of humans to create a title for themselves in the process.

One of the dilemmas of my existence is to find an organization and subsequently a label which allowed for my growth. It has been a mission of sorts to find a group of people that not only shared what I have often considered 'square peg' point of views in a 'round peg' world to feel comfortable and have a community with which to belong.

Throughout my life I have lost close relationships because of the interpretation of religious vocabulary, been subjected to abuse and told it was acceptable because of interpretations of religious vocabulary, been told that I had no right in a place of worship and that I was not experienced enough to share all because of interpretations and belief systems wrapped around religious vocabulary. I thought my mission to find a compatible place complete with the joining of and ordination in a Spiritualist Church. At present I still think that perhaps the Spiritualist title, if I am to accept a title, is the closest I can find to encompass my unique brand of understanding and vocabulary. It is the one 'religion' that I know of that accepts that people are responsible for their own paths to enlightenment. Certainly there are certain 'principles' that are accepted by most of the members of the Spiritualist Community but overall there is a unique understanding that not one person in the community may squelch another's understanding and growth. The challenge to the Spiritualist Community, as with any other religious centered community, is to not only allow the differences and the uniqueness and the understanding that all are enlightened and understand at different rates and in different ways, but also to celebrate with each other when the understanding comes to our fellow humans. We are each here in a capacity to encourage enlightenment in each other. We share our unique stories, we share our unique feelings and thoughts, we come together to share in community. We also need to come together in rejoicing in each other's Divine Spark. We also need to remember that to achieve understanding and knowledge we need to LISTEN. We need to BE STILL and we need to JUST BE. We need to allow for the expression of love and UNDERSTANDING. We need to celebrate in each other's journey and be willing to learn from each other. We need to be willing to take this imperfect language, to listen as best we can to other's imperfect use of this imperfect language IN LOVE. When this is done we become enlightened ourselves. When we listen and share in such a way that the door is opened to our neighbor to understand beyond the boundaries of ritual and dogmas we have also stepped though our own door of understanding.

"And the greatest of these is love." (I Corinthians 13:13). Love will transcend all of the language differences. When acting out of the knowledge and understanding of love acceptance in each other and where they are at right here and right now is possible. When speaking out of love it is possible to transcend language and create a place for UNDERSTANDING. When sharing love it is possible to start to be love. It is possible to allow the part of ourselves that was created from love to remember where it came from. It is in the complete stillness, absent of thought, words, language in which the awareness of that love permeates into our humanness. We once again, for a tiny span of time, reach the Divinity we are all expressing in our unique way with the language, vocabulary and dogmas. It is in continually coming back to that stillness that will allow the love to permanently permeate our humanness. It is then that we realize that even with a label we are so much more. We realize the labels may be necessary for our world dynamics, but they are not necessary to grow and allow those around us to grow in the UNDERSTANDING of the completeness of the love found in the dark part of our being, hidden away in the deepest part of our human condition. IN the stillness the darkness is no longer scary. In stillness, in the absence of any language we see the spark of the Divinity within ourselves. The spark that will never go out, but can be fanned into overpowering the darkness when we take the time to JUST BE. Allow for the knowledge that we are MORE than flesh, we are more than thought and we are so much more than the cumbersome use of words to express the overwhelming love that is available.

To JUST BE we admit we are more than the label. To JUST BE we allow for others that are on different parts of the path to fade as we encounter new ones. To JUST BE we allow for that spark of Love to fill the entire pathway encompassing our human reality of past, present and future. We acknowledge that in the traveling we learn, in the struggle we grow and in the allowing our true selves to shine, to JUST BE, adversity will not wane, but it will no longer hinder our ability to know and share love.

12 GRATITUDE

(Written Nov 2013)

November seems to be the 'traditional' month of being 'thankful'. There are posts on the internet, there are prayers at a Thanksgiving feast, there are clothing, food and toy drives to gather from people that have 'more' for people that have 'less'.

I took someone very dear to me to one of the meditation and QiGong classes I teach a couple of weeks ago. She had a beautiful experience during the meditation, and felt a lot of loving and cleansing energy during the QiGong motions and exercises. She was very, very quiet on the way home, which, really isn't all that different than other times, so, I didn't pry, I allowed the silence and we went our separate ways after returning from the class.

It is in the silences that we most often find our most poignant truths.

It is what we allow ourselves to hear because of the silence that can allow those we serve to teach us more than we are teaching them.

My young friend confided later that the experience of class had touched her very deeply. She asked how she could achieve such peace and happiness and such a state of healing again without me present.

Indeed.

Without me present.

That is what it is all about, isn't it?

Serve, teach, share in such a way that those that have come or asked or are put on your pathway for a little while to be able to go and understand their own way of finding peace and community with the Universe.

We talked about how being thankful for everything, even things we may not have quite achieved is very important. That in being grateful we train our minds, our energy, our humanity to remember that we are so much more than what we see in the mirror. We understand that we are spirit wrapped in flesh and not flesh trying to obtain spirit. We are already there. When we are thankful NOW our spirit is able to shine NOW and when a light shines it can light up the darkness.

In response to our talk a little poster was made with a list of everything my friend is thankful. It has been put into a frame and is hung where it can be seen every day. The last bullet point said thankful for Jenn.

It is hard for me to even type that without tearing up. Thankful for me. To know that each and every day in a frame someone has decided to be thankful for me and send that positive energy my way is humbling, and beautiful.

I also received a message from the same person very happy that since the list was made people around don't seem to be as moody or down. There is a realization that the mood we each put out and the thankfulness we each put out has an effect on each other. The light or the darkness we decide to emit DOES indeed spread and effect the world around us.

It is about the little things. It is about that one person we can touch, that one person we can serve. It is that personal contact. It is very wonderful to donate this time of year. It is necessary to share our food, our extra clothing and toys with those who do not have any. It is necessary to remember ALL we are thankful. It is also necessary to spend that personal time. Hand shake, smile, hug, phone call, a note.

In our entire lives if we touch, truly serve and help JUST ONE soul to find their own personal connection to Light and shining their own unique version of that Light, we have had a successful life.

I am thankful to my young friend for reminding me that we are able to touch each other in allowing and being comfortable with the silent moments

I have a thank you list that I go down each and every night. I actually keep it tucked under a pillow so as I lie down I remember to be thankful, even if I have not taken the time yet that day. There are special people on that list; there are things like my car, and money and the clients and students. There is family, and the gifts that Spirit has given. There are seemingly silly things like my camera, computer and cell phone (which has not only helped my business grow but also has kept me in touch with some very special people). There is my church family and my Spirit Circle family. There are things added each night depending on what happened during the day. Remaining thankful and sending that thanks right to Divine has really, really helped me focus on what is important. Focus on NOW. It has helped greatly in my CHOOSING to be happy despite obstacles, trials, lessons and heartache.

It has helped me greatly look forward with a tremendous amount of HOPE.

13 PRAYING, ASKING, WISHING, THANKING

Praying for guidance, wisdom and strength
Praying for insight. *(Prayer written while things seemed very dark and bleak, a praying for guidance from the depths of a soul, my soul, which at the time seemed very lost)*

Praying to understand when to step in, speak up and when to tame down.
Praying for those in mourning, and those transitioning to the Light of a life without the physical body.

Praying for those who have been or are being bullied.
praying for those who do not understand that their actions are considered bullying.
Praying for those who have the courage to speak out.
Praying for those who stand their ground.

Praying for patience.
Praying for safe travels and good times for those away from home.
Praying for those who have to drive in the snow.
Praying for those with no beds, or hats for their heads.

Praying to understand what it is all for.

Thanking Divine Love for this day.
Safety, smiles, and Despicable Me, a movie which brought out
4 year old giggles, wrapping the house in glee.

Thanking for friendship, children, family and husbands who are
doing well.
Thanking for friends who stop by and check on him, and
though gift certificates send us out for a spell.
Thanking for knowledge, and students and the ability to care.
Thanking for jobs, and freedom, and cars (even though they all
need repaired)

Asking to keep seeing us though.
Asking to remind me not to worry about the medical bills,
insurance bills, tax bills and living bills.
Asking that guidance is there and a glow on the correct path.
Asking that I remember to take time to Breathe, Pray, and
Laugh.

Wishing well, friends with birthdays this week and day.
Wishing well to those who needed a hug today.
Wishing apprehension to fade. Wishing God to understand all I
cannot say.
Wishing feelings running so deep, to God I offer all to keep.

Angles are here every day, surrounding us, whispering to us,
helping us on our way.
I saw one this week, almost as plain as can be. My friend, she
said she prayed for help as the same time I saw, beside her all
the help she would ever need.
Wising for the same strength and an angle of my own, and I

continually feel like I am traveling into the barren unknown. The White Light of Heaven is always near, is always there shinning. I know this, I feel it, I ask for its healing and protective touches every day for myself and those I love. To totally trust it, and allow it to guide. To open myself up to listen to the message inscribed by it on my heart, this part is often hard. For I know as soon as I totally surrender, there will no longer be excuses in the realm of faith and belief. Why have I not totally surrendered? Can any of us totally surrender here on Earth? Can any of us really be the small child running to the parents arms: totally trusting that all will be well once in those arms? I am ready for peace. In the quiet spaces, please show me how.

14 HEALING

Healing is one of those words that end up in a jumble of people's perceptions and experiences. In effect it is very loaded word.

The very first "doctors" in our human communities were considered 'healers'. They had various titles such as 'witch', 'shaman', wise man or woman' etc.; in some areas they were considered the wisest of the wise, the ones in the community and society that innately knew what to do for their fellow man in terms of practicalities in the herbs or natural remedies of the region and also because of an ability to sense and channel energy to where it was needed. Once industrialization and 'civilization' made way through technical advancements humans started not 'feeling' as they once did. There was not always recognition that the energy around us, the same energy in the trees, in the plants and animals and indeed in the earth itself is the same energy that is in each and every one of us. ALL of creation, ALL of the universe was created from the same exact source, and effectively connecting it all.

Hands on healers are not a new phenomenon. How some perceive hands on healing has changed though the millennia. Religion and the age of needing to have a scientific answer to what is taking place both have underscored the need for reeducating, especially the western society, on the nature of healing.

There are a multitude of studies out at present, available at the click of a mouse button on any internet browser that will talk about the power of positive thinking, will allow for an understanding of how using ancient methods of QiGong, newer methods such as Reiki and even the all-inclusive label in the power of prayer have merit in maintaining wellness in humans. These studies have once again given validity to the power given to each and every one of us to tap into healing.

The question then comes to the forefront as to why there is still illness, disease, and atrocities like cancer if we are able to tap into universal energy for healing?

The simple answer is that there is a clear distinction between healing and curing. In our society the end is what is considered the important step in any situation. Getting the diploma, the job, having a successful marriage, and beating things like cancer to go on and have a 'successful life'. The END is not always the answer for our personal path and growth.

We each one of us here are here in order to learn what is unique for each one of us to learn. Not one person on earth came or was sent (depending on your point of view). Healing energies is a way, a tool and beautiful and loving gift from the Universe to help us each upon that path of enlightenment.

I am a healer. I have always been a healer, although I did not recognize it in those terms all of my life. The instinct to KNOW what a person needs on a physical, emotional, and/or spiritual level when they need it is a sign of a healer. The person, who if takes the time to recognize, innately prays or sends others energy and Light even if those specific terms are not used and finds that people are better (emotionally, physically, spiritually) because of the contact is a healer. The person who sits with another and says nothing but is a presence of peace at that moment and at that time is a healer.

There are many of you reading that will be nodding his head in recognition of one or all of the statements above. We ALL have the capacity for healing ourselves and each other. Some of the capacity is in the will, some in the acceptance and some in the willingness to acquire a knowledge base through schooling or training, meditation and practice.

There will be many that will claim that no one is able to heal as Jesus healed. This may be certainly true, but not because Jesus was the only capable healer. Jesus had the beautiful KNOWLEDGE and UNDERSTANDING of how totally linked we are to the Spirit that created us. Jesus' pubic success in healing as instantaneously and powerfully as has been recorded came about because of the total and complete trust he had in what happens when Spirit is directly involved. He was also working with a community of people that as of yet were not bombarded with the non-reality that medicine was the ONLY answer to any type of physical and emotional dilemma.

Yes, the views of the individual accepting healing are just as important as the healer.

A healer, whether claiming a modality such as Reiki, QiGong, or Spiritual or no modality at all other than connectedness taps into the great universal constant of Love.

Love in the form of Spirit and Energy is all around us all of the time. We were made of it, the earth and universe we made of it. We are the FREE WILL manifestations of life created from Love. In order for us to fully understand this love it is necessary for each of us to struggle in some form. In some way we chose to be here at this time to learn and understand how to become closer to Divine Love. To learn there needs to be a quandary. In effect, we play out the most complicated story problem in an effort to solve for Love. In each and every story problem there are variables, quotients, and even a story itself. One must not only attempt to understand the story but also understand which variable to solve for and when so that the other part of the very complicated expression may be completed. Part of the story may be loss, disease, hardship, depression, disagreements, and financial issues. Fortunately for us there is a Universal Calculator with a Healing function that smooths out part of the story and even helps to eliminate some of the variables. In healing a balancing of the equation can take place, even if for a short time, to allow for processing and enlightenment because of and in the midst of the problem solving.

A skilled healer is able to help a person balance. A skilled healer is one who allows for Spirit to work and also so speak through the healer in the best interest of the individual accepting the healing. A skilled healer knows that sometimes the time spent with someone is a brief time, sometimes only one meeting and it is enough information and experience for the person at the time. She knows that some people will call for help when there is an immediate issue physical or otherwise for some type of relief and release from the issue. She also knows that some people still need to be met with again and again for the process within them will be a slow one. She lastly knows not to judge the process. Just as one's path is not the same as another's neither are the needs for healing nor balance to maintain a footing on that path.

This is sometimes the hardest but most important thing to express while teaching others the validity in healing, especially when teaching self-healing. EACH and EVERY soul is different. For some healing will mean a 'cure' and for others a balance of love and acceptance and possible patience. For some healing will mean that they are able to touch and know Spirit in a way that was not possible without the need and the want to know and learn healing. The pathway in healing, which even though some may need to go through for their own healing and enlightenment, that needs to be avoided it the learning and using of healing for own personal gain in the areas of notoriety and earthly wealth.

Compensation is something discussed in each and every one of my healing classes. It is understood that it is necessary to have some type of energy exchange for the information and the knowledge, the time and the experience of a teacher and healer. What is not understood is that the knowledge and way of knowledge for someone seeking should be kept from them because money is not as readily available to some individuals as others. In this society the accepted energy exchange for any type of transaction is money. There are some that legitimately do not have the funds at a particular time and a particular place. Healers and Teachers of healing need to be aware of the needs of all. Keeping open to the one individual that may benefit the most and then turn around and help the most people from your ability to understand that there are other form of energy exchange is one way in which love and understanding is spread.

This is one of the reasons that many will travel to a church setting for their teachings and for their healings. There are many that are great teachers and have great success in healing that are completely out of reach in terms of monetary exchanges for some individuals. This is not to say that a teacher needs to undervalue themselves. To do this would not allow for more people to learn, it would only allow for the teacher to them not be able to make a fair living either. There does need to be a willingness to have a conversation with an individual that is a worthy student for a delayed or even different type of energy exchange (different than money).

In the United States society a person is more respected, and is more apt to receive employment if there is an actual piece of paper like a certification or diploma. It is necessary to in effect go to school to not only learn more about one's chosen craft but to also hear and learn from those with practical experience in the area. The opportunity for me to earn one of these papers in the area of QiGong while my family was struggling financially because my husband undergoing cancer treatments. I did not formally sign up for the class even though the instructor knew that I was ready for such a class and such a step. He approached me and simply said "you will send the money when you are able." I took the class and almost two years after the class I was able to send him a check for the time and experience he shared with me.

Recently I taught a spiritual development class. One of the students that had attended another series of classes I taught was not in attendance. When I left the classroom, I found him in another room sitting alone and eating his lunch. When I asked why he had not joined us, since he was already there, he said that this month was tight for him and his family (he had just become a new daddy) and he did not have the money to attend classes at this time. I told him that he would have the money when he had the money, or he would discover something I needed in trade, either way, he was still welcome to sit in on the class. Of course every single instance is different than the other, but if there is a true desire for one to discover more, travel deeper and be a part of a spiritual development process the lack of money need not be an issue. These things always seem to work out.

I have been at open events where I would offer a chance to touch Spirit though a short healing. There are times that some came to discover and experience and left no donation and then others who leave more than what I would ever expect. When you are being both true to yourself and to Spirit the means to the end will be shown. The ability to continue will be available. It is our responsibility to continue, to take advantage of the opportunities that allow us to keep growing ourselves and also to make sure we and our families are surviving to continue.

There are many people that serve Spirit and serve Spirit well that choose to do so in their "free time" away from their "paid work environment". There are other people that have decided that serving is their full time mission. This is a huge choice. This is also one in which the individual serving must work hard to not only serve but maintain a life for themselves that is filled with Spirit.

It is impossible for any of us at any time to fully take care of others, to be a bright beacon and to serve Spirit to the fullest is we are not first taking care of ourselves and our own relationship with Spirit. This is most of the reason I insist on teaching those that are new to Spirit or those that would like mediumship training that Healing training comes first.

The first thing an individual learns is to become still. Each class a different type of meditation is explored. We need to understand how our own bodies feel to be still. We need to understand how it feels for us to sit in the silence with Spirit before it is possible to effectively link with Spirit or allow Spirit to use us for Healing or Mediumship. We learn how to ask for, channel and receive self-healing. In the self-healing process we learn what it is within ourselves on a physical, emotional, mental and spiritual level we need to shed and heal.

I have students that will remember things that happened to them as a young child that they are still carrying around the guilt or hurt. Others learn where they carry stress and anger, how to identify it and release. There are others that learn what the warmth of Spirit and Love feel like for the first time and they learn how to accept such feelings allowing them to grow. It is totally impossible for us to effectively help each other if we are not aware of what we need to work on and care for in ourselves. We must be willing to take care of our physical, mental, emotional and spiritual bodies. When we understand how we feel it will help us when given cues in others. A competent healer will recognize feelings he has discovered while working with himself as cues on how to help direct energies and counsel to others. Healing truly starts with one's-self and it is a never ending process.

Daily practice in meditation, healing, energy work like QiGong, eating sensibly and even walking and going to the gym are all necessary for our spiritual growth as well as our physical well-being.

QiGong has been mentioned many times because that is the energy, healing and physical system that I gravitate. Each and every person will find what works best for them. I teach a wide range of modalities because each one in essence tackles relationship to Spirit in much the same way. The end result is the same. There is merit to Spiritual Healing teachings, Yoga, Reiki, QiGong, Oneness, etc. It is in the feeling, the knowing and the striping away of the labels that one will find what works best for them on their healing and spiritual journeys.

Eckhart Tolle teaches that it is best not to "name" a thing. He says it is better to "call" a thing. When we place names on the energetic and Spiritual healing styles we add to it all kinds of cultural and religious connotations. This is really unnecessary. The feeling, the result, the healing is the same. One must be willing to try and even "call" the practice something different if that helps the process. For example: there is an exercise in QiGong in which one "nourishes your qi" . There are many people that have a block when someone talks about qi (chi). Depending on who I am teaching I will tell them to absorb energy, nourish your Spirit, allow Spirit to work with you, and/or float in the universe. The person learning and the person in need of healing will feel what they need to feel, the process will work the same as it did when I learned "nourish your qi" only the vocabulary is no longer in the way for the person working to receive benefit.

When working with others, it is IMPERITIVE that one does not get hung up on the phrases and words that others use or even we use ourselves. Take the time to really LISTEN to what is being said. HEAR the meaning behind the words not just the words themselves. Often the educational, cultural and/or religious backgrounds of people get in the way of the healing that is available.

Healing is one of the greatest gifts Spirit has available for us to use daily to keep a balanced and healthy and also to aid in perceived "miracles".

Intention is EVERYTHING in healing; the intention of the healer and the intention of the person who is being sent the healing. There are some things that healers do that are very physical in nature. This helps our very human side. There are techniques of touch, techniques in which some healers use sound bowls or sound tuners, techniques that involve crystals, dowsing rods, pendulums, scents and symbols. These techniques work with our physical nature. We like to see and feel that something is actually being done and accomplished. We like to know that someone actually did something during our time with them and for some healers they identify with the "tools" listed above and they mentally help direct their intention. I find more and more that the tools are alright to use, when the intention is a pure one. There are some of my clients that I will touch more than others. There are some clients that really need to see that I have a certain crystal in the room before they feel comfortable that Spirit is working. There are other clients that want to be sitting, or laying a certain way. There are some that I will share QiGong or pressure points with and give them homework for themselves. The more a healer works the more her own personal intuition and link with Spirit will become apparent. The more a healer gathers in information and practice the more she will be able to pull from that information to be able to be of a specific help to the individual who has come to them for healing help.

Healers will receive the entire spectrum of people that need assistance. I have personally have clients that have depression issues, loss issues, physical ailments such as Lyme disease and Parkinson Disease. I have had some clients come because they wanted assistance in recovering from surgery, clients that wanted to be rid of cancer treatment symptoms others had certain pains that they wanted rid of and others that had something as random as an eye growth the doctors did not know what to do about.

I have clients that come once or twice and what they were coming for is no longer an issue and I never see them again, and other clients that I work with long term. There are still others that only come to group healing sessions in which there are many people offering each other healing and love at the same time.

Each and every case, each and every person is unique. Spirit working with these people is unique. In the process of physical and or emotional healing a person also travels down a Spiritual Path. A person understand their body more. They have the free will to accept or not accept what is being offered to them during a session. They have the free will to accept or not accept the suggestion of meditations, exercise, and/or reading materials during a session. When a person is willing to work with Spirit, then the healing will take place.

Healing is different than a cure. A person seeking and working for healing will ALWAYS get what is needed. This is not always the perceived WANTED outcome. For example: an older lady suffering from chronic pain and discovers through her healing process that when she is more active and spends time with her grandchildren her pain is decreased. It is up to her to make a few changes in her life to go with her healing process. Healing is not passive.

My husband did not receive a clean bill of health from his healing treatments. Actually, early on, he was getting better, the cancer was receding. It was suggested that he continue certain mental exercises, get plenty of walking and sunshine and also continue his healing treatments at the rate of about once a week. It was suggested to him that it was possible to get better, but it would be an incredibly slow process requiring much work and stamina on his part. This lasted for a tiny span of time before he decided finding some type of pill would be better for him and he stopped his QiGong healing treatments. About a month before he passed he asked again for the healing treatments. This time, even though the physical part was not 'cured' there was a definite spiritual healing that took place.

When it comes to Healing it is ALWAYS in conjunction with a traditional medical source, especially when the issues are physical in nature. There is no need to choose one or the other as my husband felt the need. Spirit allows for free will and also cognitive thinking. It is amazing what the human brain has been able to learn and understand and it is a good thing to tap into that type of expertise. Partaking in Spiritual and Energetic healing only heightens what is available. There has to be willingness and a trust of Spirit on both the healer and the person asking for healing for maximum benefit to take place.

It is not magic. It is the power of intention. We wield a LOT of power with the thoughts in our brains. It is impossible for us to not affect each other with our thoughts and emotions. When people that have decided to be in a 'bad mood" they spread that throughout their day. The reverse is also true. Choosing to look on the "bright side" and choosing to know that this moment at this time is really all we have and we need to make the absolute most of it permeates our reality. When we have a mindset of Love that love is spread. That is the energy that is released during healing. The joining of one individuals love with the Love from which we were made and then that love being shared through thoughts, hand on experience, distance sending and intention that the highest and best be accomplished for the person in need. When we understand that the other human understandings and modalities and the way of teaching others how to feel Spirit working are beautiful ornaments on the tree of endless LOVE.

15 CHARLIE

(April 2013)

For the past few days I have been 'stranded' at home because of a sick baby. (Well, he is four years old but he reminds everyone that will hear him some days that he is indeed "Mommy's Littlest")

It has been incredible beautiful out the past few days as well -- up to 70! Woo HOO! Around here, the way it has been weather wise lately -- that is an absolute blessing!

Instead of playing full speed ahead we have had to take it a little bit east and sit instead of play in the sun.

I guess, sometimes the only time this house slows down is

when one is ill. I just made out the calendar for the next couple of weeks and we have track meets, sports banquets, kindergarten sign ups, trips to the doctor for Galen for testing, academic testing for kindergarten and college, work - of course, fundraising events, 5k running events, a 'child' turning 21, pre-school trip to the zoo, symphonic and jazz concerts, and I do have tickets to see Rock of Ages soon.... looking forward to that.

Sometimes I wonder if it is all too much. But, if we were not busy, if I were not busy -- what else would I be doing?

I literally cannot sit for very long. Some preliminary testing Lloyd had for college came back with remarks like ... very active, possibility for short attention span. When asked specific questions Lloyd said that he thought his mother had some ADHD issues -- HAHA! I guess the boy knows his mother, just a little bit :)

While classroom teaching -- and even in the general public -- I seem to have an affinity with the 'special' children/people that may not quite fit the 'norm'. So, I am not sure why I even try some times to even make this house and family -- 'normal'.

And who is to say what is normal?

I saw this earlier this week and sent it to a friend recently.

> A friend told me that I was delusional. I almost fell off my unicorn.

Her response was priceless -- she said she preferred her delusions over their realities

YEAH!!!

So -- ADHD? Phewwy! This family is just full of a bit more faerie dust than some may find comfortable :)

And as for the schedule -- well,... since most of that has to deal with the children there is no way it is getting changed. Starting Kindergarten and finishing high school will only ever happen ONCE.

Beginnings and Endings -- Endings and Beginnings. They really are just opposite sides of the same page. Have to have one ending before can get to another beginning --

And I am not sure all endings are really endings, anyway.

More like doorways, chances to learn and grow.

The doorway the last few days for me was to learn to sit a bit more than usual in one place, with a little one that needed someone to sit with him. -- for the first day the thought actually ran through my mind that I was getting nothing done -- look at that extreme list that needed prepared for, look at the laundry and such that needed completed -- look, see, ...

But I was getting something accomplished. I was sharing healing, I was sharing love -- I was rejuvenating myself just a little by actually taking a nap with the little bugger.

My reality will never be the same as another. Another's will never be the same as mine. Neither will the delusions.

My unicorn's name is Charlie -- he is a very lovely animal, a bit smaller than most allowing me to climb on bear back by just jumping and holding onto his rainbow colored mane, while sliding onto his velvety shimmering white back. His hooves are a bright purple and his eyes are a lovely crystal blue with dark green eyelashes. When we ride the fairies follow offering glittering light through the darkest of tunnels ... through the most chaotic of days, reminding of freedom of thought, the preciousness of children and the wonderment of the Universe.

16 POURING LOVE

I have heard many people say that when it rains -- it will soon pour. Many people expect it to pour. Often this is a negative comment. I know this can be a positive.

Many people bring on their own negative pour through their own actions, fears and insecurities. I am just as guilty as anyone else in this matter. It is so easy to listen to people hurting, see friends going through a time of health issues or emotional turmoil and wonder what the heck the universe is thinking. It is so easy to become so afraid of repeating past mistakes that you even sabotage good things that have come your way out of fear.

I have a friend that constantly reminds me that fear is
False
Evidence
Appearing
Real

How easy it is to subscribe to the idea that everything sucks so why not just let it.

How hard it is to pick a small thing - anything - to be grateful on a day that seems intent on bringing us down.

How easy is it to choose thankfulness over despair?

Light the Darkness with choices of Love
Light the Despair with offerings of peace
Light the uneasiness with a knowing of more.
Attract Light by remembering you ARE Light
Spread Light by uncovering the reality inside

Refuse to sink to the human created
despair
drama
depression and unknowing

Be silent - hear the truth within

The truth of unending Love ready to carry you above everything this world may throw your way.

CHOOSE
Choose to be Thankful
Choose Trust over Worry
Choose Knowledge over Ignorance
Choose Forgiveness
Choose Light

BREATHE
Breathe in Goodness
Breathe in Light
Breathe our Despair

KNOW beyond a shadow of a doubt that creation is LOVE. We came from Love. We will return to love and it is a choice in this existence to feel, know and share that love. It is OUR choice. It is OUR learning experience. EVERYONE has the choice.

We live
We attract
We love
We are well or not well
We learn or do not learn based on our OWN choice on how to receive, spread and be of service to the love of Creation and Divine.

We radiate what we say
We radiate what we think
We radiate what we do
We radiate how we love

Ripples of what we radiate traveling to the horizon and beyond.
Ripples merging and touching with the ripples of others.
Ripples merging with those of a similar frequency and love.
Ripples merging and spreading.

Decide for yourself which ripples you would like to merge. Forget about what is perceived by others. This is your learning experience. This is your time to grow.

TRUST
Trust when you act from love and truth and
Trust when you serve from love and truth that Spirit will always be there to guide and provide.

Light of Spirit surrounds
Sounds of Light permeate
Love of Light shines
We are Light - sparks of Love from the Source of all love
We can soar on truth and love
-Trusting
-Breathing
-Loving
-Knowing by connecting
-Knowing by listening to the silence deep within

Ecstasy in the silence filling those who listen with more love than can be contained in this physical form. Love that must be shared - Pouring love - Rippling to the horizon and beyond

17 MYSTICS DREAM

There are a lot of times that it is certain lyrics that strike me for the day, or ones that I would like to convey. This time it is the entire piece of music: Mystics Dream. I placed the lyrics after this section.

There is something about this story starting in the evening -- in the beauty of the moon. A crescent moon. A moon that is growing and changing.

There is something about the birds calling in the morning. A song that allows for a new day, a new beginning.

There is something about moving from the "earthly" night to the LIGHT. A light in which it is possible for the energy of the heart and LOVE to move the stones.

Love to be sure in all things -- to be shared in the "earthly" part of our existence and the "spiritual" part of our existence.

The "lamps" the Light calling home. Always. And yet in each and every breath. In each and every "earthly" night we are capable of feeling, learning and loving. In fact there is no other way while we are here, until we are Home.

Sometimes it is hard to reconcile our nights and our days. It is hard reconcile what we know to be a part of our soul with what is going on in our everyday very "earthly" lives. It is hard to remember that both the Sun and the Moon are indeed a apart of our personal realms of existence.

There is a meditation that I frequently use in the middle of QiGong classes in which we envision both the sun and the moon energies blending and then also blending with us. We become whole, well, and much more a part of our existence when we remember that we are a blend of all around us and are willing to take the best of what is around us and create the best possible blend for us, our walk and our understanding. Blending the 'opposites'. Blending the 'past' with our very unique 'present'. Blending our own often 'voiceless song' in the Light that is always there for our upliftment. Finding love, knowing solace and eventually encompassing peace.

Lyrics to the Mystic's Dream as sung by Lorenna McKennit

A clouded dream on an earthly night
Hangs upon the crescent moon
A voiceless song in an ageless light
Sings at the coming dawn
Birds in flight are calling there
Where the heart moves the stones
It's there that my heart is longing for
All for the love of you
A painting hangs on an ivy wall
Nestled in the emerald moss
The eyes declare a truce of trust
And then it draws me far away
Where deep in the desert twilight
Sand melts in pools of the sky
When darkness lays her crimson cloak
Your lamps will call, call me home.
And so it's there my homage's due
Clutched by the still of the night
And now I feel, feel you move
Every breath is full
So it's there my homage's due
Clutched by the still of the night
Even the distance feels so near
All for the love of you.
A clouded dream on an earthly night
Hangs upon the crescent moon
A voiceless song in an ageless light
Sings at the coming dawn
Birds in flight are calling there
Where the heart moves the stones
It's there that my heart is longing for
All for the love of you.

18 SILENCE

I hear a lot of people complaining. I have caught myself a couple of times with a huge sigh about to emerge because there are boots and hats and cleaning off of cars and walking trepidatiously as to not fall flat on one's rump.

What it is doing, however, is keeping the world.

Quiet. Winter is quiet. For those of us that experience a real , snowy type winter the blanket of white stuff acts as an immediate sound dampener. People stay inside more, the animals find places to hibernate or stay warm, I do not even hear much out of the neighbor's dogs through the snowy months. Sure, there are play times in the snow, there are get-to-gethers and there are winter sports, but on the whole it is much quieter than the rest of the year.

A bit of a reminder I guess to just SLOW DOWN. A reminder to take time to LISTEN to not only the world around us but the people in our house and also the sounds that come from deep within ourselves. Allow ourselves to go silent. Turn off the music, the TV, the devices once in a while. Take the time to just be.

It is easier to do that when it is winter.

It is easier to close out the world, sit wrapped in a blanket and allow the mind to go blank ... giving permission to the Divine that dwells within to have a conversation with us.

So often even that conversation is a loud one. We do all the talking and complaining and wishing and spouting off wants and intentions and whys and what ifs.

How often do we take the time to JUST LISTEN.

It seems fitting that the snow is hanging around during the week before Easter this year; certainly one of the few times that many churches insist on a little silence. This is especially those who have services all week of different themes building up to Easter Sunday. You do not have to be a part of one of

Christian Traditions that do have services all week, or even of a Christian tradition at all to appreciate that God does indeed dwell in all of us and would like to spend some time with us ... in the silence.

Scary as silence may be -- and it does take us a bit of practice.

Yeah, the snow can drive one little crazy. Greenery is more pleasant to me, I want to play in the dirt, I want to take the kids to the park while I do my running/walking and sometimes even meditating. But I will savor the moments of nature's silence in the beauty of a white covering for a few more days. Reminding me be still sometimes, reminding me patience.

KNOW beyond a shadow of a doubt that creation is LOVE. We came from Love. We will return to love and it is a choice in this existence to feel, know and share that love. It is OUR choice. It is OUR learning experience. EVERYONE has the choice.

We live
We attract
We love
We are well or not well
We learn or do not learn based on our OWN choice on how to receive, spread and be of service to the love of Creation and Divine.

We radiate what we say
We radiate what we think
We radiate what we do
We radiate how we love

Ripples of what we radiate traveling to the horizon and beyond.
Ripples merging and touching with the ripples of others.
Ripples merging with those of a similar frequency and love.
Ripples merging and spreading.

Decide for yourself which ripples you would like to merge.
Forget about what is perceived by others. This is your learning experience. This is your time to grow.

TRUST
Trust when you act from love and truth and
Trust when you serve from love and truth that Spirit will always be there to guide and provide.

19 FAERIES IN THE GARDEN

I have a friend that constantly tells me during discussions that one only has as many faeries in the garden as one puts in the garden. His point is that one has as many falsehoods and unrealities as one are willing to accept.

The first time I heard this phrase in my direction I noticed myself becoming irritated, and decided to let the discussion drop. I mean, really, who is it to tell another person if her fairies are real or not?

The second or third time I heard the expression aimed my way I believe I responded with a resounding "Well, I like fairies?" Which, in fact I do very much. I like their stories, their drawings, and their mystery quality. I like that there are stories of good and bad faeries and that a lot of the moral dilemmas faeries face, even with the gift of magic, seem very much like the ones humans face. Faeries appeal to my Celtic heritage and they are lovely stories to share with the children while on hikes and while planting the garden. There is a wonderful faerie garden in Lily Dale where people leave trinkets both for the faeries and for their loved ones that have passed. This place is filled with the air of possibilities and love. I like that about 5 months before Dean passed into Spirit that spirit presented itself to Dean in the form of a golden faerie. He talked about finding peace and love in the vision of the faerie. When he looked for alternative treatments to his cancer far from home he would tell me that he thought the faerie traveled with him to be a link to home while he was gone. I never saw his golden faerie, and yet I am forever grateful to Spirit for working with Dean in a way that was both comforting and peaceful to him at a time when he had very little of either.

While I was thinking about why I like faeries it occurred to me that a person really does have only as many faeries in the garden as one puts there. It also occurred to me that no one else has the right to take away from that person what any of those faeries represent and mean to them.

Our personal gardens, our places of growth are totally individual. One person may be drawn to pebbles and desert type foliage while another has a more oriental garden while yet another has a vegetable garden and their neighbor a tropical one. Those gardens will change over time. I am sure that some people have gnomes in their garden, or reptiles and others have foxes, eagles or even fluffy bunnies. There are also the fair amount of them which will have faeries. They are as real to them as the eagles are to the person with the western landscape garden. We each have the correct garden for us at the correct time. Depending on how much we are willing to attend the garden will determine just how many climate regions are able to be represented or if we are a specialist just how full and perfect our chosen climate has become.

I am one who gravitates towards many climate regions. I think a garden is fullest when the best of all of the regions available are gathers in one place and find a way to thrive together through cooperation and sharing of the resources available. I find I am a better gardener when I understand how other climate regions work and even how specific gardens work in each of the regions. This allows me to have an easier conversation of discovery and understanding and mutual growth with another. I certainly believe the faeries in my garden are the absolute best. I also know that from time to time some of the old plants need weeded out and I may lose a faerie or two in the process when that change happens. I may also gain a different type of faerie when I gather new insights and information.

Each and every plant, each and every ornament and indeed each and every faerie are there for that person at that time and it is indeed needed for the completion of their garden. I do not think it is for me to say to another if they have too many or too little of anything in their garden. I can merely offer my point of view, my guidance on what works for me, and my garden and it will be up to them if they try any of my advice or not.

Take the time to learn all you can. Become the best gardener you can possibly be in your own garden. Take the time to be still within your own unique garden. It is only then that the best gardening secrets and treasures are revealed. Don't be afraid to swap plants, stories, treasures and even...faeries.

20 WE ARE ALL CONNECTED

We are indeed particles of the Universe rearranged in such a fashion to join with our very unique life force for a short span of time. Our bodies, this fleshy substance that aids our spirit during our human existence is pulsating energy. Each section of our body can be felt and even viewed with different types of medical equipment in different lights, spectrums, wavelengths – essentially energies. In the western world of energetic learning we know some of these areas as chakras. We have identified seven of them on the body. There are some that would say we have 9, the 8th and 9th one or the 1st and 9th one depending on your point of view being slightly elevated above our head and other one slightly below our feet effectively linking our energies to the world and indeed the universe around us.

In the India a system known as Prana healing is taught. They also acknowledge 7 chakras (although they are named differently and have slightly different colors than the west) They also talk about our five energetic bodies and how they relate to Divine.

In China, where QiGong is taught, there are three main energy centers of the body called Dantiens. These are the upper middle and lower portions of our body. These make up our physical energies. There are also Universal, human, heaven and earth energies that are felt taught, mixed and aid in the communication and energization of the physical Dantiens. There is also a realization in the healing aspect of QiGong that each organ and each energy pathway of the body (which is knowledge that is taught and tapped into by acupuncturists, acupressure therapists and even some chiropractors)

It really does not matter which energy system one chooses to learn, discover and use as a basis for his own growth. Whichever one or whichever blend of any of the above or the many more available on the planet one chooses Spirit will work with you in that manner to allow your knowledge of healing and of energy to grow. Spirit will tap into those pieces of knowledge, which become little energy signatures of thought in your brain and Spirit can blend with that energy to help in guide you to further discoveries, developing your energetic and healing intuition and also think of those pieces of knowledge in ways that perhaps you had not thought about before.

This in itself is a form of Spiritual Development. Any way one furthers in communication and understanding when working with Spirit is indeed Spiritual Development. One does not need to be a member of a church or an organization to be very spiritual in nature. In fact, some of the most spiritual people and ones that have done the most good in teaching others about their own path did not associate themselves directly with any type of religion. In fact all religions, even the one that I have been ordained, are flawed in their human approach to Spirituality. We gravitate towards one religion or another because of the human need for connection and community.

LIKE does indeed attract like. Those that have a similar moral structure, that maybe have similar backgrounds, that have decided that they need validation in some way for the way they are feeling and thinking. This is the nature of religion. Where it becomes unnecessary for growth is when we buy into the notions that some religions have about the distinct right or wrong way of being, thinking and feeling. When what one has for breakfast, what day a service is attended, which verses of which specific book are acceptable as teaching are dictated instead of explored then we have lost touch with our own personal relationship with Divine.

To be spiritual is a pathway of discovery. It is learning how our energy fits with the energy of Love. It is learning exactly what love is in all it many unending facets. There is no church on the planet that can dictate the exact methodology for someone to discover those things.

What a church has is a group of people that have decided to help others on this discovery by fully immersing themselves into their own discovery. The sign of a good church is one that will allow a person to come in exactly how they are and not try to CHANGE them in any way. The sign of a good church is one that has a great amount of opportunities for learning and growth by its members in the form of classes, lectures, demonstrations, healing and community events. A great church is one that allows and rejoices in the discoveries made by the community that meets together under the heading of that church. It is one that recognizes that everyone is discovering at his or her own rate and creates an avenue for information, experience and higher level thinking while never knowingly causing one that may not have felt something someone else has felt to feel anything but love and complete acceptance for who they are at this particular time.

One unique way to open the pathway to your own discoveries is to explore those energy levels within yourself. If we take the idea of the seven chakras and that the first chakra is our crown chakra we take some time to understand that within that chakra is our physical link to the Divine. There are many that feel a tingling in that spot when they are connected to Spirit either during meditation, as a medium giving a reading or a healer during a healing session. Take some time right now and be still and quiet. Close your eyes and allow your jaw to relax and drop. Draw your attention to your breath, how deep it is, the rhythm, the space between the breaths. Widen the space between your eyebrows. Smile. Listen to the deep silence within yourself that is waiting each and every second of your day to be heard. Allow yourself to feel the warmth of the sun above your head. Allow yourself to feel its rays warm as a July day radiating down in the center of your crown. Allow yourself the knowledge that the sun is concentrated energy of the Universe. It warms, it energizes, it allows life to grow and develop. Spend the next moment or two in the realm of no thought and yet the complete warmth of Universal energy.

■■■

This is the energy center which is activated within us when we just KNOW that we are all connected. This is the energy center which connects us to each and every single atom and wave of energy that is available to the universe. This is the energy center which is described to feel the energy before it reaches the rest of you and before intention of spreading to another during Spiritual Healing. This is the energy center in a QiGong healing session in which the practitioner will connect with first, asking for energy and light to enter the client though this region before being sent to the central meridian or other sections of the body. This is our energy compass. This is the place in which ourselves, our uniqueness and our individuality and indeed our sense of entitlement as an individual collide with the truth that we are ALL part of the same Universe. We are all a part of the same breath of life and indeed we are all a part of the LOVE that we are trying so hard in this human form to explore. Sometimes we do a better job at it than at other times. Sometimes it is easy to remember that we are all capable of love and even deserve love from each other. Sometimes it is easier for us to believe that we are entitled to do well, have a better position, receive more clients, have a certain network of friends, we feel that we well, are just better, or know more. Sometimes this is a healthy thing. Really. It is good to understand oneself, it is a good thing to acknowledge one's gifts and what one is good at. When it becomes an issue is in the realization that we do have a gift and that we do pretty well at a certain subject or task that we no longer have anything to learn from it or anyone else when we are involved in the thing in which we are good at. It is when we are in this state of consciousness that we are no longer involving our energies with those around us. We have separated our energies. We have retracted the Divine Spark that is in us into the very center of our cavities.

This also happens to some of us when there is a life crisis. For example in my own life in the time leading up to Dean being diagnosed with cancer I had started to withdraw from the world around me. I knew there was something very wrong and instead of acting on the instinctive knowledge that I was being sent by Spirit I decided it was best if I just kept to myself and kept plugging away. This was a lesson I had not yet learned from the time of my first marriage. When I became very aware of just how wrong things were for me in that marriage I chose not to say anything to anybody. I chose to withdraw into myself and just 'handle' the situation. There was a fear on my part in the communication. There was a fear in what people would say and how they would react. There was a fear in what was happening at home would become worse if others knew. I was brought up in a family that did not talk about issues that the family was having. That was considered no one's business. It was also seen as a way to protect others in the family from knowledge that may be hard to hear or hard to understand.

This type of culture was so prevalent in my family that I did not know that my parents had a baby born to them before me that passed of a birth defect known as spina bifida shortly after it was born until I was in my early teens. I had another very large experience with this type of information withholding when I was 21 and pregnant with my first son. I had an uncle which was very dear to me. He and I would hang out in the summer when I visited my grandparents, and he was one of the few people as I was growing up that I felt completely comfortable around. He would talk to me, share his likes and dislikes, introduced me to music, and would 'guy watch' with me through my teenage years. My uncle was gay. This was something else that was not talked about. In fact so much not talked about that I remember attending his wedding when I was young and then overhearing my grandmother talk about it later once the marriage dissolved and how she wished that she had talked about that aspect of his life with him more so that he did not feel obligated to become married as he had. My uncle was sick on and off for a few years. I was told that he was sick, that he was in and out of seeing doctors, but I was never told that he had AIDS. He attended my first wedding. He and I danced. I have some very nice pictures of he and I together. I had no idea at the time how very sick he was. Something in me expressed the need to send him a package one day to share with him how much I thought of him. I put a book in the package of a movie I knew he liked very much, a letter and a few other trinkets. The package was returned to me a short time later by my uncle's partner. He had passed. I wonder sometimes if I knew just exactly what was going on if I would have picked up the phone and called instead of sending the package. I wonder.

It took me a while in the beginning of Dean acting weird and being sick and feeling the strain of his not feeling well at home to remember that keeping things hidden is NEVER the answer. It didn't work when I was young, it didn't work when my uncle was sick, it didn't work while I was going through difficulty in my first marriage, why would I think it would work now? This is NOT Spirit working. This is ourselves and our inclination to not stir the pot that was at work. We sometimes are fearful of other's reactions, what people will say about us and the family and what the changing result may be in our lives when we are open and honest.

We are unable to draw strength from others, and the powerful energy that entwines us all if we are not open. This does not mean to say that we need to share all of ourselves every day with everybody. It does mean that we should be true to ourselves and admit when there is a situation that needs help and healing from others. This is our human connection. When we allow for this human connection to happen the honesty, the openness, the sincerity will bring forth energies in others to help us accomplish what needs to be accomplished. This is the free will part of our journey. This is the choice. Do we allow for a mingling when it is necessary, or do we believe that only we are able to further ourselves.

Do we recognize that we are ALL here for each other? Do we recognize that we are indeed connected to each other, the energy in the spring flowers, the energy of the falling snow, and indeed the energy in our thoughts. ALL connected. When we realize that we are indeed a part of each other our entire existence and our entire world changes. When we allow the energies of love to enter we attract others who have done the same. When we allow for the expression of "I don't know what to do now." Those who we have connected to with love spread out those thoughts, those positive reinforcements in the way of prayers and conversation to allow miracles to take place.

Once Dean was diagnosed, against the wishes of Dean, I allowed everyone to know. He at times was so against other's involvement that I made it about me and the children. After year one had passed in his diagnosis Dean started to talk to people on his own about his illness, but this was a new thing for him to do, for he was also taught that people did not talk about what was going on in the family. Allowing myself to be connected changed that experience totally for me. I know I could be very bitter right now, I know that my family could be in terrible shape in terms of food and finances. The positive thoughts, the well wishes, the positive energy people sent our way in both physical and non-physical ways made all the difference. That I accepted the exchange of energy from these other people validated their need to send love in whatever way they thought necessary and helped them feel what sharing love is all about. That spot on the top of my head, the place we refer to as the crown chakra was full of tingling energy. I was able to know when something was about to happen directly because of someone's or some organization's goodness directed our way. I look at a lot of those people and institutions differently than I may have before. I see what they have done for this family. I see how seeing us as a part of the human community that needed love created a healing environment and even though that part of my pathway was by way the hardest I have traveled as of now, there was a peace about the whole process that would not have been available had I not allowed my 'personal space' to be invaded by so many others, many of whom I have and will never meet face to face. I have a very unique understanding now of how we are all connected and how it feels when we allow ourselves to be connected. It is possible to feel that when we are open to it on a daily basis. Allowing for the complete quiet space and the space in-between thoughts and breaths, the space that is sometimes so completely dark that we know only the Divine Spark of Love can light it up is the key to discovering this feeling...this knowing. It is in being completely and totally present. Eckhart Tolle calls is being in the NOW.

Saint Theresa of Avila calls it being within the interior castle – the very center of our being which was created first, where our sense of Divine and Love resides. Sometimes the feeling only lasts a nano second, but in that nano second the realities of a Divine Intelligence connecting all creation through Love is powerful. That nano second allows for the complete love, respect and acceptance of the rest of the individuals that add their essence to the energy soup we soak. It is in this energy soup we become most aware that although we are individuals we draw the most strength and flavorful outcome when we swim in and draw from the community of Love.

21 WE ARE ALL ABLE TO FLY

Light of the Universe unfold
Touching greatness both large and small
Light of the Universe knowing
Gentle and True
Lighting the pathway
Lighting the walk of growth
A Light that never fades.
A truth that always rings
Binding all energies, all time and all love.
Feeling Divine Power
Knowing Divine Love.
Nothing is impossible.
We are all able to fly .

22 CONNECTING TO SPIRIT

When we admit, express, share and develop love we understand a tiny bit of the substance from which we were created and are all completely a part. Mediums have the awesome responsibility and the incredible honor to be a physical connection bringing forth tangible evidence of that love to console, to guide, to help grow the understanding that life is never ending and that love never dies.

Mediums are a special kind of person that is able to link with Spirit and have a personal relationship with spirit. A medium is able to FEEL and KNOW that Spirit is there with love and guidance.

YOU are a medium.

There are different aspects and type of mediumship. There are the mediums that sit with others, or are the ones in front of a congregation during a message service or in some other type of public setting in which a medium public demonstrates the continuity of life by bringing forth loved ones of the audience members.

There are some that would argue to bring forth proof in the continuity of life is the most important aspect of mediumship. This aspect of mediumship is something that I work with and practice with Spirit on a daily basis to always improve. This is the aspect of mediumship that is really the most public. Mediums stand up in front of a group of people to give a message. The message which states that Spirit knows that you are struggling with an issue at this time and is with you and wants to let you know that it will get better is a very nice message, unfortunately this is a message that everyone is able to receive and deliver. There is not one of us that is not struggling with something at some time and would like to be told that it is going to get better. This same message prefaced with specifics about the spirit messenger that is there to bring forth love and support in the situation will not only bolster the validity of the message, but also bring forth some proof to those who may be skeptics that life really is continual.

There are some mediums that would go as far as to say that if there is no evidence of who the spirit messenger is then there is really no message at all. This same line of thought may be drawn out further to include that if the message ends up being from a guide or a spirit messenger that is not readily recognizable by the person receiving the message then the message is also not valid.

I struggle with this strict interpretation on how and when Spirit can and will communicate with us here in the physical world. There are an entire series of books called "Silver Birch" in which the guide whose name was identifies as Silver Birch speaks though the medium Maurice Barbanell for many years offering advice, and wisdom to a great many people who came to sit in circle with him. This spirit communicator did not have any direct connection with any of these people. He simply chose to come back and work through a medium to teach and offer guidance to those who would listen. His messages on love, commitment, perseverance and mostly trust are amazing and inspiring.

All of that being said, I do understand the limitations of a message and public demonstration service setting. In these and times in which a medium works there are many skeptics, there are people that may be experiencing mediumship and Spirit communication for the very first time. In these instances it is most imperative for the medium working to have an actual connection with Spirit. One way in which to prove that the connection is real and that Spirit is indeed with us with every turn is to bring forth that evidence. Allow the person for which the message of hope and love is being offered know exactly which loved one in Spirit is around them still and bringing them that love. It is important in these cases for the medium to work with Spirit in such a way that the message is as specific as possible. Perhaps the medium describes the physical appearance of the person, the physical condition the person was in at passing, a shared memory or even tidbits that shine through the loved ones personality. When these items are described BEFORE one is told that there is a struggle and that it is known about and that there is lots of love and support for the situation the message then becomes real not just for the intended recipient but also all those in attendance. The message not only brings forth love for recipient it also allows the entire room full of people to understand that we are continuous and that the love shared by people here does not fade with a passing but in reality grows beyond any measuring capability we have at present.

Mediums that work in this fashion, in front of the public, have an incredibly awesome responsibility. It is incredibly necessary to keep their own personal issues out of the way so that the message from Spirit is clear and precise as is possible. These mediums also need to work daily at quieting themselves, in taking care of themselves in such a way as to maintain a good vessel for Spirit to connect and also remember that they are in SERVICE to Spirit. None of this is about the medium at all. It is about Spirit sharing with us and reminding us that we are not alone. It is Spirit coming back from the place of pure love and light to remind us that is indeed where we have all come from and where we all will be going and that this place at this time, even though it is all we have and all that we are able to learn from at present, is not all that there really is. We are more, the universe is more, love is definitely more and we have the ability to connect with that reality through a medium.

Mediumship also takes the form of private sittings and consultations. In this setting a medium will sit with another in a conversational type setting. The medium will link with Spirit and become an opening for the person seeking to touch with Spirit.

People ask to speak to mediums for a variety of reasons. There are some that have had a loved one pass that they would like to connect. There is loss and grief and a need to be sure that the loved one is not lost. I have sat with people in this situation. The ones that are most memorable to me are the ones in which I did not know that was the reason for their visit and request for a reading. I have started instructing people to not tell me right away why they have asked for a reading. In this way I know that Spirit is the one guiding the process and that I am not trying too hard to please the person sitting in front of me. The last thing any medium should ever do is to not be true to the message that is being given.

There was a time shortly after my husband passed that I chose not to do readings for others after church service but instead sought out a reading of my own. I could feel my husband around, I could pick up on clues that were happening in my everyday life that let me know that he was there and never very far, but I was having trouble actually hearing, which was frustrating to me since when I sat and connected for other people I was able to 'hear'. I sat with a medium that knew my husband had passed. I respect her abilities very much. In fact she was one of the very first people I officially talked to about specific training for my own abilities and how to train myself to work with Spirit better in order to help more people. This other medium, however, allowed some of her own personal issues and thoughts interfere with the message that was being brought forth for me. She said, "I hear what is being said, but I would like to tell you in my own words what I think it means." She had gone through a passing of someone very dear to her two years prior to sitting with me that day, and the sting of her own grief seeped through into my own reading; so much so that she changed the words she was hearing to fit her own personality and situation. I was devastated. I wanted to hear MY MESSAGE. I wanted to hear my loved one's words, personality and feel that love. I learned a valuable lesson that day. I learned that it does not matter at all what I think the message means. It does not matter if I would not use those images or those words. It does not matter if it sounds completely ridiculous to me, especially when Spirit shares with me metaphors for another. My interpretation of images, words, metaphors could be and probably is completely and totally wrong. As a medium it is my responsibility to share what is being given. The more specific, the more clear, the more precise the better, but the message for someone else is NOT for me to change in any way. I would never want to make someone feel as low as I did after that reading. The reading in which I had hoped would be able to release some of the frustration and grief I was feeling ended up being one of complete frustration. I will never know what Dean had conveyed at that moment that got changed. I will never know what part of his personality may have revealed something else for me to think about or to simply smile about and remember in the times grief came creeping.

I also learned that it is VERY important for a medium to be continually working on her-self in order to properly serve others. It is VERY important for self-healing to take place constantly in any form that works for her. It is important to sit with Spirit frequently, so that the connection, the energy and the feelings are more recognizable and clearer allowing for us to trust in stepping aside more and more and allowing Spirit to shine for others in the way Spirit would like to shine; all without out cumbersome baggage to get in Spirit's way. We all have free will even in the realm of a sitting. The medium can very well choose to leave out part of a message, change the wording, and the sitter may choose to believe or not believe what is being said. The mitigating circumstance to the negative is that the sitting takes place from love. Love of the medium for her work, and for her fellow human and love from the sitter in the form of trust and the openness to understand.

Earlier I said that YOU were a medium. Does that mean everyone is in a position to offer messages in front of a congregation or even in a private sitting? No. Those instances take extra training and a willingness to give over part of all one's life in the service of spirit for those particular types of serving. What it does mean is that everyone is able to know, grow in and train themselves to understand Spirit's cues in their life. Everyone is able to connect in some fashion to spirit and have an inner knowing about Spirit's love. There are many that train to be healers that have a beautiful connection with Spirit that helps guide them to help others during healing sessions, counseling sessions and also though the distances of physical space. This type of mediumship is beautiful and valuable.

I have a beautiful friend that is more connected that anyone else I have ever met. She will be the first one to tell you that she was not always this way and that it took a lot of work on herself to heal from early life situations and anger in order to be at a place of connectedness. She is a spiritual leader in every sense of the term. During healing circles she is able to channel direct words from spirit, often times poetic in nature that hit the person emotionally exactly where they need to be hit at the time. She is one that completely understands that everyone is on a different area of the path and often we are all traveling different paths in all of the different gardens mentioned in an earlier section of this book. There has not been a time with myself or another that I have heard her say that our relationship with Spirit and what we were experiencing was not a valid one EXCEPT when she understood that a person's experience was more wrapped up in their own sense of entitlement and the stroking of their own ego than a true relationship with Spirit. She has helped people that the medical establishment had deemed in need of medications realize that they were in fact not crazy, and just sensitive to all that Spirit has to offer. She understands that some people will see guides, and other angles. She accepts the need for tools, props and above all the complete unconditional love needed for growth and change in a world that often looks crazily on people when their eyes are opened in such a fashion by Spirit that many things do not matter the way they once did. She exudes an inner strength and knowledge that seems both simple and completely ancient in context. She listens before she speaks and if she does not have an answer she asks for a day or two to meditate on the answer. She is fully aware that her guidance for others comes from Spirit. She is not afraid to say she does not know and then spend time with Spirit for guidance in the answer. This is not the mediumship that we often see in our western world. We see the private readings, we see the public demonstrations, and we sometimes seek spiritual counsel in those readings. I know that I have had many people come to me for a combination healing and spiritual guidance and I need to link with Spirit during my time with them to fully understand their needs and offer guidance. These clients of mine may not take kindly to me saying, "I hear what you are saying, and since I do not want to give you false advice I need to be given a day to meditate and sit with Spirit before I guide you." And yet, sometimes that is the total and correct answer. She has taught me total trust in Spirit and the process like no other training I have received and I am a much better healer and medium because of that advice and teaching through her own actions. There are times when I do tell others that I need some time before I offer advice on a type of exercise, meditation or even life situation. I have found that the complete honesty in saying that right now I just don't know and I would like to take time in the answer has been received much better than I would have originally thought.

I also have learned not to sugar coat anything I may be given from Spirit. Spirit loves, Spirit is all forgiving, and Spirit will certainly tell you, if you care to listen, when you are getting in the way of yourself. Spirit always allows you the choice. That is our part that is our free will. A medium in a position to help another or a medium that is feeling internal guidance for herself will always understand that the choice in any situation is totally ours to make, but the decision to take the path to further our relationship and growth with Spirit is the one that our Spirit communicators will cheer for. For myself, those choices always seem to be the more difficult to make, but also the ones with the larger lessons.

Understanding our own mediumship qualities and the type of communication that is possible with Spirit allows us to fully touch and understand that all-encompassing unconditional love. For many of us our first mediumistic experience may not be one in which we see loved ones that have crossed, it may not be a near death experience, and it may not be full knowledge of our guide or guardian angel. For many of us it will be that still split second in-between breaths where the world becomes incredibly still and in sharp focus for the first time in our lives. It will be the time we see a butterfly land on the tip of a flower right in front of our eyes and we feel connected to that time, that space and indeed that butterfly. We take in the moment, we become a part of the moment in a way that allows us to know in the core of our being that we are a part of so much more than our everyday activities. We find in the first breaths of a new-born baby we helped to create that life itself is much more than a jumble of cells coming together ... it is love. Love so deep and unfathomable that in our humanness, wrapped in language it would take us much longer than we even have on this earth to express the depths of the love we have experienced in those in-between moments.

It is in the in-between. It is in the vastness of that love. It is in the willingness to spread our personal energy this and merge with the universal energies which create the soup of creation that the blending and exchange of the different aspects, tastes and textures of that soup take place. It is in this exchange that mediumship happens at whatever 'level' or 'experience' it needs to take place. We each have that capability. It is a choice on how much information we would like to allow and train ourselves to receive from Spirit. It will depend on the choices of how much to serve and in what capacity. Spirit will take its cues from you. It will allow for communication at the level at which first you have an innate gift for and second at the level you train yourself. That part is our free will. Once the choice has been made Spirit will be there for the rest.

23 MEANING OF THE SEASON

(Written December 2013)

You don't need to believe in **Yule**, the Scandinavian fertility god, to enjoy the tradition of Yuletide carols and greetings.

You don't need to be a **Wiccan** to enjoy the tradition of wreaths or decking the halls with holly.

You don't need to be a **Druid** to enjoy the tradition of hoping for a kiss under the mistletoe.

You don't need to believe in the god **Saturn** to enjoy the tradition of decorating a Saturnalia tree in your home.

You don't need to believe in **Thor, Odin,** or **St. Nicholas** to enjoy the tradition of a visitor bringing gifts at night.

You don't need to believe in **Sleipnir**, Odin's flying 8-legged horse, to enjoy the tradition of listening for the sound of hooves on your roof top.

You don't need to believe in **Mithras** to enjoy the tradition of celebrating the sun's rebirth on December 25th.

And you don't need to believe in **Jesus Christ** to enjoy the tradition of renaming this ancient holiday to Christ's Mass.

All you need to enjoy these winter festivities is to be merry. **Merry Christmas**

TRUTH SAVES
www.Truth-Saves.com
atheist-overdose.tumblr.com

I found the above photo posted online. I do not know anything about the organization that published the reminder, but I do appreciate the reminder very much.

I struggle with the holidays every year for a variety of reasons. This year it is a combination of my little ones being incredibly weepy with the idea that their daddy is not here physically to enjoy the holiday festivities with them and the pressure we place on ourselves to have gifts for each other. There are toy drives and food drives and activities for all kinds of charities around. I have chosen a local firehouse this year that has a 'Breakfast with Santa' day to take my children. The money for the entrance fee and activities all goes to the volunteer fire department. It also allows my children some fun. The other activities, are just not possible this year with a tight wallet.

I wonder about my own choices and then consider the people that do not even have a house in which to be in this Christmas. I have that. I have a paid for house because of money sent to us after Dean's passing. Also a great gift. A gift that I find that others do not have. I know of a young single mother who was recently forced to move into her parent's living room because the cost of working and day care to work had become too much to also afford living expenses. I know of other families that are dealing with loneliness because of loss, cancer, the possibility of MS, and others with financial issues. All in this season when it is supposed to be the brightest, the most filled with hope.

All though our human existence we needed reasons to

celebrate at this time of the year, at least in the northern hemisphere parts of the world. It is literally the darkest and will remain so until after the winter solstice. It is the coldest, it is the time when activity slows and bellies sometimes get a bit plump due more to inactivity than anything we may or may not be eating. Now place the consumerism and the pressure of making sure it is a Merry Season, especially when one has children, and the season can be out right painful.

My Christian friends will tell you that the birth of Christ is the reason that they celebrate this time of year. For them it is a world of hope brought to them in the form of God made man.

For me, there is a realization that in this darkness, stillness, and sharing through charities and parties and families coming together that for some reason we as humans need a season and a reason to remember how we can be all year round. Perhaps this season is in this time of year because it is so dark and cold and it gives us a wonderful excuse to do all these wonderful things. Unfortunately since it is THE TIME of the year, the ones that are not able to participate for whatever reason sometimes feel less than adequate. I also hear and see people bickering about the 'real' reason to celebrate and do kind things and get together with friends and offer gifts to one another. Really, does it truly matter?

My son had a little 'Santa's Workshop' at school earlier this week. He was to take money to spend on presents that he got to pick out for others. We made a little list of the people he may want to give to and we found some money in our household piggy bank to put in his envelope. Up until that point this season I was very melancholy myself about the whole culture of gift giving this time of the year. I had been receiving invitations to attend and be a part of toy and food drives when having those things for my own family was in question. He was soooo excited about the opportunity to shop FOR OTHERS. He came home explaining what he got and for who and how proud he was that he would be able to share those things at Christmas. He, even though he had a little money left over, chose not to buy anything for himself that day, only for other people. He is 6. My brain has been working overtime on how to keep this spirit alive for him ALL YEAR long.

This morning he and his 5 year old brother were up ridiculously early. Well before 6AM. They were in their room with paper and colored pencils and pens creating a little book of pictures and designs. I could hear them cooperating, enjoying and deciding just how big "Best Mom Ever" would be written on the cover. They needed something to be under the tree for me.

I have heard many times that children are on this planet to teach the adults and not the other way around. This has certainly been true this week. As the Grinch finds out it is the size of the heart that matters. NOT what religion you are, if you even subscribe to a particular religion, the external reason you are celebrating, where and how you understand your traditions. It is the complete sharing of the heart. LOVE always wins.

Special thanks to my little ones for the beautiful reminder. Enjoy your season. Love and Light be yours and be shared by you.

24 LOVE NEVER DIES

It is in this existence, this solid form, this human flesh that you are able to learn all that it is possible to learn about returning to the land of Light – you are absent of the brightness of the light from which you came – but that bright light is available to you at any time you wish to receive its guidance.

Humans act as if they are totally encased in darkness. There is turmoil, there is despair, and there is worry and fear. There are people worrying and creating their own dilemmas by creating fear based energy out of the trivial matters of human existence.

To know that there is always guidance from the Light is to know that these things are merely to learn from. The trials of today are the groundwork of discovery. The worries for the day called tomorrow are non-existent. Why worry about what may or may not come? Time is irrelevant. It is today that is strategically important in the makeup of the learning and comprehension necessary for development. It is in the present moment where the tiniest sensation, the tiniest sound or lack of sound, where the tiniest breath, spontaneous hug, drifting of thought all takes place. It is possible to miss these tiniest of things in the midst of worry and fear. We will miss what it is we came here to learn and understand.

We will miss that we have never been disconnected from the light – we will miss that we have nothing to prove to get back to the light. The Light will ALWAYS be there as will the LOVE that the Light represents. We are here merely to grow. We are here to understand how to share and develop love. We are here to bestow the gratitude of love on each other. We are here to support, to learn, to grow to serve humanity in the best way possible in spreading this love. We are not here to worry, to have fear, to question our tomorrows.

Tomorrow is a total figment of the imagination. In the Light there is no tomorrow – there is only this very moment. Time is not a linear structure. Time is a structure invented by the thoughts of human mind to attempt a structuring of our reality. Our reality here is only a commercial in the middle of the show of the Universe already in progress. Our reality is a break from the existence of spiritual development in which there is always unconditional love.

"You don't know what you got, till it's gone" is true even for those who were born into Spirit with the breath of Creation. How do you express love? How do you understand love? How do you accept love? How does one know if one wants to be in an existence of love unless one is subject to the possibility that there is not any love. We experience either directly or indirectly loneliness, disease, poverty, despair, depression, pain, jealousy, hate, greed, injustice, abuse, and the struggle with personal identity. We find that these experiences are choices. We find that these experiences can make or break our willingness to accept love. We discover that we may choose to love anyway. We find that when an outlook of acceptance on the reality that these things are learning tools and not rules of the universe. We discover that the effect of the experiences are lessened and our progress of development and learning becomes easier. We find that where we are all at a specific time and completing a certain task is THE MOST important moment. We find that if we are always looking for a time when the negative experiences will end so that life will become better, or a time that once a task is accomplished or a material amount is procured in a bank account is reached then life on this planet suddenly becomes grand is a total false notion and not the reason for this existence at this time.

This existence is transitory. This existence is a manifestation to what we REALLY are. We are soul, we are spirit choosing to be wrapped in a fleshy existence to connect to the Universe and all it has to offer in a way that would not be possible without this existence. We learn, we grow, we teach we love. We take that love and the knowledge of what it feels like in the lack of love back to the Land of Light. We develop further there as we review what it is we have learned. We decide if we will help others and how we will help others. We communicate back to the ones we love who are still a part of the earthly world in signs, dreams or communication through a medium to give support, hope and love in their continued learning experience. We express that life does not end. We help our loved ones remember that they too will return to Light AFTER their period of learning and growth.

Humanness is an important step. We are in effect the Universe, tiny sparks of Divinity graced with the gift of free will determined to decide for itself if LOVE really is the answer.

It is. More than any of us during this moment will ever be able to realize. To feel that Love that resides deep inside of us connect to the Spirit that has never and will never leave us to totally fend for ourselves in a moment that will carry any type of incredibly dark situation in your life in a way in which you as a person are not destroyed. To understand, to receive a tiny glimpse of the Love that is waiting to fold its arms around us when we return Home and realize that it is indeed to wrap us up at any nano second of the day if we still ourselves and allow ourselves the luxury of keeping ourselves in the present is to understand that the greatest of all the gifts of the Universe is indeed Love. Seeing and feeling everything totally draped in that love totally changes the way in which you react, act, speak and think about the people, events, space, situation and universe around you at any given moment.

We understand that our thoughts are a projection of Love or total lack of Love. We understand that our thoughts, words and deeds all have power and the energy to build another up in love or totally destroy them and essentially ask them to rely totally on themselves and their link with Divine to overcome anything someone else may throw in their pathway.

We all know people that are terribly capable of doing just this. Nothing seems to faze them, ever. They seem jolly, well centered, and poised. We also know some that will outwardly show these things and break apart when alone. We know that we are sometimes flawed in our approach to others and situations. We understand that we make mistakes and sometimes act in reverse of love. This is the learning process. The challenge is to minimize the mistakes at every turn. The challenge is to understand where we need to grow and work towards that and not to be afraid to ask forgiveness and to offer thoughts of love to those who in their learning processes are unloving toward ourselves. Love is shown most through adversity. This is where it shines and is a reminder of what is possible.

We spend time with Spirit. We spend time in silence, we spend the time. We take the moment and we relax in spirit, connecting, allowing the exchange of energies and love. We remember who we really are and who is really there helping us through this learning process.

We remember that it is LOVE way more than life that never dies.

We try really , really hard to live out this experience and even to share it with others once we have this incredible experience and realization ourselves. Once an awakening takes place it is incredible hard to even think about going back to what once was.

It is possible to have many awakenings in your life. Little sparks of intense knowing that allows for growth and a glimpse at what life really is. I know that have had many. I have had experiences alone and with others that have allowed me to understand that in this grand universe there is so much more than what we see on the surface of our human 'life'. A lot of these times were in the quiet. They were times in which the world slowed for a little while, in which the moment became so incredibly saturated that the minute details of the depths of feeling can be remembered and carried on in perfect clarity into the rest of our lives. There was a time I sat in a dark church when I was sixteen years old. The birth of each of my sons, times on walks where it seemed nature had taken a hold of my senses and for an instant stopped the world from spinning and I was indeed connected to the energy of the world.

I traveled to a workshop/retreat this past October (2013). Before My husband passed into spirit we had talked several times about me attending this two week event and further my training and understanding of healing and how healing works. This workshop was run by Master Robert Peng and taught QiGong healing. The first week of the event there was not only learning but also a cleansing. As we learned and worked on each other and ourselves we started to understand what we needed to heal in ourselves on all levels. There were many there that wanted to learn how to physically heal themselves or a loved one, there were others there on a spiritual type journey and understood the way we work with Divine in the area of healing can further that experience along and make all the difference in spiritual ones spiritual development. There were some in the class such as myself who were already practicing energetic and spiritual healing and working with others and there were some that were experiencing this type of healing for the first time themselves, as well as sharing the healing process with others.

I remember feeling lighter and lighter as the first week progressed. The energy of the class was amazing, the people were all very loving and sincere, and I had found in myself in working with the others that I not only could feel and know where I needed to be to help a healing process, I was also hearing guides and loved ones, and seeing internal structures of the body. I was very used to and comfortable with just knowing. I would know what exercises and meditations to have people do after a session, I would know how often I may need to see them for whatever issue it was I was helping them with at the time, the explicit instructions from Spirit and the visions of what we being changed and healed was new. I was starting to feel connected like I had never felt before.

There was one practice session where my partner was directed to work specifically with my lungs. I could feel the energy moving there, I could feel my lungs being filled with the energy in the form of love that was being offered. Then I felt as if a tennis ball was being removed from my lungs. My partner said he felt like he had a solid mass and the energy did not feel as if it were healthy for that region. He grabbed the tennis ball sized of more dense energy and took it out. I felt myself gasp for air and I saw flash through my mind many of the harder moments I had experienced the past few years with my husband including his passing moments. QiGong teaches that the lungs will energetically hold joy and they will also energetically hold grief. If we do not deal with our emotions and release them they become a part of us and it is then harder to deal with. Healers are no different in sometimes needing help to release such emotions. My partner was taken aback. He asked what it was that he had felt, was I alright, for my then I had streams of tears flowing from my eyes. I explained to him what happened so he understood if he ever encountered something similar again when helping heal another and thanked him for trusting his intuition.

I spent a lot of time alone that day. I spent a lot of time totally void of thought on the breaks from class. On my way back to my van that evening to drive back to where I was living those two weeks I saw a figure in my car. There was someone in my passenger seat, and at first I was frozen as to what to do with a stranger in my car. The person turned and I recognized him as Dean. He smiled, and then he was gone. Gentle acknowledgement, for me, that even in releasing some of the grief I was not going to lose his presence in my or the kids' lives

A couple of days later I was with some other healing students on break at a lake area at the retreat center. We were lounging, taking in the incredible warmth on and October day and just enjoying being. One of my classmates turned to me and asked if he could offer me 'deeksha'. I asked him what that meant and he said it was a way to share Divine Love. After all the other clearings, feelings and openness of the workshop I couldn't think of one reason why I would turn down an opportunity to share in Divine Love. He asked me to sit on the edge of the chair I was in and he stood in front of me and placed his hands on my head. There were people all around us. The group we were with were not phased at all by the sharing taking place in front of them. I found out later that many of them had already had a similar experience of sharing while at the retreat center. I could hear the people; I felt the breeze, the warmth of the sun, and the complete absence of any fear or worry. I felt as if I was floating in a place in which time and space did not matter. I felt as if I were two people, the one sitting on the edge of the chair and another floating somewhere a bit above witnessing the experience. I felt peace, serenity, connected and the overwhelming sense that nothing else was an important as the overwhelming love that was being wrapped in comforting layers around me. I am not sure how long my friend had his hands on my head or how long he shared the energy of Divine Love. I do know I was not able to move for a time after the exchange. It was as if my body needed to somehow soak up and process what my soul experienced first-hand. Another beautiful friend from the retreat grabbed me as I slumped over and held me close to her as a mother would do for her baby. She stroked my hair and simply said, "That was a pretty intense experience." It was twenty minutes before my mind and body felt as if they were once again in the same time zone and I could continue on with the day.

Since that experience it has been completely impossible for me to go through any day and not draw on that KNOWING of love. It redirects me when the human qualities of frustration and worry start to take hold. It is a constant reminder that there is so much more than we see before us. Since then I am constantly reminded that it is important for me to take care of me. It is important for me to practice the meditations, the exercises, the time with Spirit that I teach others is so important. I have found that my healing sessions and spiritual reading with others have been taken to an entirely other level. I am more comfortable. I trust in the process, I know that Spirit will guide and work with me to deliver what is important for the people I am working with at the time. I know that I need to continue my own growth. I know that even in the knowing and feeling what is available in this form, I am nowhere near that reality. I can receive glimpses, I can carry the memory, I can get back there from time to time in the quiet times I allow in sitting for Spirit. I can share the love available through and in Spirit by healing, teaching and sitting with others for spiritual readings. I can share the love available in the everyday moments of life. I can share the knowing through prayer, through smiles, hugs and simple understandings. I share the love by being willing to forgive both myself and others.

This experience of mine was not the first time I was led to understand Divine Love. It is the first time, however, that I made a conscious effort to not lose that knowing. It is the first time that I made a conscious decision to live out that experience in my everyday life and in my work with others. I am not perfect at it. I remind myself constantly. I remind myself that each end every moment is a process of enfoldment and growth. I remember to be grateful and thankful that it was possible for me to go away for such a time of peace, growth, healing and knowing.

Allow the possibility for Spirit to touch your life in a way that is moving to you. Allow the possibility for healing, growth and messages. Allow for the still moments and the non-thinking moments. Allow for the present to totally take over. Allow for that nano-second of existence when the connections between Universal energy and the Divine Spark residing within the fleshy vehicle of humanity to remember each other and fuel the spread of the Love of the Creation. Spread it through kindness, through sitting with others, smiles, listening without judgment, giving without thought of repayment, and by taking short pauses before reacting to any situation. In this way we help others to experience the feeling and knowledge of love. In this way we help each other reach those sometimes fleeting moments of our earthly existence of complete knowing that Love is indeed the answer and never, ever leaves us alone.

25 COMPASSION

We are all filled with more understanding and an incredible sense of what each other needs. We all, if we take the time to focus, are able to pick out what each person needs without that person even taking the steps to attempt to articulate what it is that they need. We know.

The solar plexus region of our body is the one in which the chakra system will tell us in our emotional center. It is located between our heart and our abdomen. Centered in our body, able to feel the ripples of the physical cues the rest of our body may or not be sending out in any type of situation. It is the part of us that reacts, that brings in the energy of compassion and knowing for others. It is the part of ourselves that we need to be aware of to balance our own emotional needs and pressures.

Our energy is unique. Our energy reacts and sends signals to our brains for processing each and every time it reacts. Each and every time we react we have the ability to understand a little more about the world around us and indeed the person sitting right in front of us. It is in this inner listening that our compassion rises.

What is compassion? It is the ability to sympathize on the level of instinct with another. It is the ability to tune into another's unique reference point and the inner knowing on what they need at the time. It is the innate knowledge in us that helps to even out the energy of others, if they allow. Compassion is the choice to respect another for where they are at any given moment. It is the ability to allow others to know that you do indeed "get" where they are at and are willing to accept them, anyway. It is the strength to allow those who we are compassionate for to know that they do not need to stay where they are at if it is a low time. It is the strength to allow others to know that you are willing to send light and healing. It is the strength to listen, lend a hug and even arrange some extra help depending on the difficulty, but also to let them know that emotions need to be released. Emotions need to be identified and dealt with, not held onto. Rev. John White is very fond of saying in his workshops and lectures that we all have emotions, we all deal with emotions, and we do not need to BE our emotions.

I recently did a workshop for a management group of an organization. The topic was how to take responsibility for one's self, totally. It was a conversation on how our energy does indeed touch and affect others around us and it is our own decisions what kind of energy we are giving off at any given time. We talked about how one may feel an emotion; one may be sad, or happy. One may feel anger or joy. We talked about how this was so much different than saying "I AM sad." Or "I AM angry". We are NOT emotions.

Eckhart Tolle speaks of grief. He talks about how his parents both passed within a couple of months of each other. He recognized the sadness, he wept when he needed to, but he also accepted the situation for what it was. It was in the accepting that he was able to move past the grief.

There are so many that I work with that have so much trouble moving past the grief ... any type of grief. There is one lady that I have worked with on and off for a couple of years. Her daughter passed from an accident and left her as unbalanced as any mother would be after the passing of her child. There is unwillingness in this person to move forward. During my time with her I understand where she is at, I convey that to her. We have had sessions in which we talk and others in which we completed a hands on healing session for her. There are moments of clarity after the healings, she sounds much like her 'old self' and yet, it is a choice somewhere within her to not move forward. She stays within the grief and it has consumed her for three years. She confided recently that she still had trouble answering the phone, for she knows that her daughter will not be on the other end of the phone. In a lot of ways she has become her grief. Her life had become her clinging to the memories of her daughter and the toll it took on her family. At some point, even in understanding that she needs to be heard, that her grief needs to be released, and knowing that she needs the company of others, I need to remember that it is not my responsibility to 'fix' her. In compassion, in that overwhelming feel of connectedness she is offered Light, she is offered Love but she is not offered the ability to bring me down into her sadness.

This is the hard part. To be compassionate to ourselves as much as we are showing and offering compassion to others. In the understanding, in the energy exchange, in the listening and the hugs we need to remember that we are NOT responsible for another's choices to either BE or FEEL their emotions.

Feeling emotions we understand, we release, we say what needs to be said, we learn and then we move on. We bring ourselves back to the reality of love. We bring ourselves back to the reality that we are able to be happy if we choose to be happy.

Being our emotions leaves us open to all realms of negative energies including physical ailments.

There has been an interesting study recently about the power of positive thinking. The Mayo Clinic has a published article on their web site siting how positive thinking can reduce stress and improve one's health. Turns out the energy in positive thinking and the chemical make-up of our physical bodies stays in such a fashion that the processes that fight off both disease and depression are heightened keeping us in better mental and physical health.

Releasing the negative energies, the negative emotions allows for the positive ones to take hold. When we remember to have compassion for those who seemingly do wrong to us through their negative emotions and reactions we help ourselves to keep a positive footing. Compassion is love and acceptance meeting in the core of our being. Compassion is the strength to allow others to know we are there to help them release while maintaining our own positive footing. Compassion is the understanding that others circumstances are not our own and realizing when and how we may be of assistance without losing our own integrity. Compassion is the acknowledgement that no matter what the situation we each have the ability to be balanced and happy despite that situation. It is showing ourselves the same compassion we may share with another, the time and the space to accept, release and move on. It is in allowing ourselves the ability to feel without becoming what we are feeling.

26 STARBRIDGE

The more I serve, the more I travel on this Spiritual journey, the more I really wonder at the competence I have in raising children when I, myself seem to be growing and changing at a rate faster than they; the more I understand my reality and my connection with all of Spirit as a bridge made of stars.

I first saw this star bridge when I went to a special invitation only meditation evening. The matron of my church knew that she would soon need to go into an assisted living facility in order to best take care of her needs. She confided that she sometimes felt as if she was slipping and wanted to be able to give the 'next generation' what they needed to continue the work of service that she started.

We were all sat in a tiny little room in which could be made completely dark. It was within the darkness that we were led through a series of three meditations that introduced our true selves … our soul to where we had been, where we were at now and where we may be going. Without lighting in the room it was possible to focus on the voice of our meditation guide. It was possible to see vividly within my mind's eye the places and colors which I was being taken.

The knowing that struck me the most during the two hours we spent being taught and guided was that of myself on a star bridge. I have seen it multiple times sense, each time with an intensity of colors and touching of my inner soul. I stood on a bridge, made of light. The light appears to be the joining of stars throughout the universe. The bridge joins the all of me. What I was 'before' where I am at 'now' and what it is possible to grow into. At first I mistook it for a bridge enveloping the grand span of 'time' itself; specifically my time. I guess that is still a correct assumption in part since we understand ourselves and our earthly lives in terms of a linear time scale. This bridge, however, this perceptional look of my core reality was much more.

From the bridge it was possible to see the connecting lights which held up the bridge. It was possible to see connectors that had been broken, connectors of different colors and connectors that were just starting to latch on in support of the bridge. It was possible to see how the stars that made up the bridge I was standing also made up other bridges that were close by and others that seemed incredibly far away. It was possible to see areas in which the Light was stitched together with rainbow thread and other areas where the rainbow thread had started to fade in the new connections that had formed from broken fragments.

There was some light that was wound over and over again, many layers. There were other sections where the light was wound only once or twice, and yet those bonds were just as relevant as the ones with thicker bands.

I was not alone on the bridge. A being had my hand. I felt warm, protected, needed, and incredibly loved. Each time I glimpsed at the being holding my hand it seemed I saw a different face, although the energy presence was the same .

I looked at where I had walked to get to the spot I was in at that time and I had a great sense of acceptance and thankfulness. I looked to where the pathway of light could take me and I felt the sense of understanding and responsibility. I looked at all the connectors at my feet, the support beams above my head, the ties on the guard rails in front and in back of me and the being holding my hand. I realized that with every breath, with every thought, with every unexplored and pent up feeling, with every movement I made those connectors, supports and ties changed. They would become thicker and stronger or weaker and start to break. They would change colors and even directions all depending on me.

Since that initial experience I have been on the star bridge many more times. Sometimes it is during development circle that I see the images, sometimes while Sitting for Spirit or meditating, and most recently while sharing healing energy with a friend or client. I have come to realize that there is a larger star in my vision. This star is filled with incredible white light. The purest, whitest most energizing light that one can possible conceive. It is possible for me to move myself into this realm of light while still maintaining footing on the star bridge. The being at my side always an anchor. When merging with the Source of Light in this metaphorical Universe healing for others is increased, the flow of love sometimes overwhelming and carrying a tangible physical signature while flowing through my human meridians before being shared with the person in front of me or being sent healing at a distance.

I have taken to telling people that they are not only receiving healing but Light as well. The pure Love of Divine available to share when one simply recognizes and allows its work to flow.

My experience is one of a star bridge, it does not have to be yours. I have been drawn to stars, and a science fiction view of the Universe since I was very young. Spirit really had no trouble tapping into what would resonate with me to share with me the KNOWING and UNDERSTANDING on how connected we all are.

My struggle is knowing how much of myself to give to the strengthening of those that have either connected themselves to my bridge and how much to ask for Divine Light to shine up their own bridges for a maintenance check. There are so many that I know about that need help in one way or another. There are others that I am aware have made very clear choices in their lives to get to where they are now. I struggle with how much I, as a healer and a friend, help another grow past situations of their own doing. I struggle on how much one should offer to help and be there for those who are in need and how much energy exchange that takes away from myself and my own family is both necessary in being a good friend and healer . I struggle with the reality that sometimes all I can do and probably should do is add them to the list of people I ask for Love and Light to enter their lives and work as much as they allow in their life.

That is the hard reality. We are in the end, responsible for ourselves. It is correct to offer assistance and love when one can, but it is also correct to maintain ourselves and our own integrity. Part of my struggle comes from the wanting to give back for the enormous amount of goodness that was shown to this family in a time of crisis. The balance is finding a way to keep spreading the love and not become so involved in some situations that we are more of an enabler than a healer.

Stepping back is the key. We need to step back onto that realm of lights. Remembering how totally connected we all are but also remembering that the Source is abundant and is more than willing to redirect and send out some extra light in the area intended when asked. Thoughts create reality, intention redirects energies and in the end free will allowing that Light to work and brighten up the part of our lives that need it or retract until asked for and accepted.

Slow and steady, steady and slow. Take the day on your own terms. Allow wisdom to flow at its own pace -- totally right and correct for you. Take some time to just be.

We are not what we have. We are not what we are planning to be. We are not in the future. Our reality expresses in the stillness between thoughts, in the silence between breaths, in the TOTAL PRESENT. Your "I AM" is linked intriguingly with the Spirit from which we were made and manifesting PRESENTLY. Just **Be** and know you are enough RIGHT NOW.

ABOUT THE AUTHOR

Rev. Jenn Shepherd *is a proud mother of 4 boys ranging in age from 21 to 5 years old. They are inspiration and grounding and a constant source of enlightenment. Jenn is a graduate of Penn State with a B.A. in history with an emphasis in religious studies. She also graduated from Mercyhurst University with a secondary teacher certification and ministry studies. She has worked teaching both young and adults for 25 years in both classroom and workshop and camp settings. Rev. Jenn is a licensed Spiritualist minister and is a commissioned spiritual healer and medium. She is a Reiki Master/Teacher and a QiGong healer. In addition to seeing clients and sitters Rev. Jenn teaches students how to develop their own energetic healing system by taking the best of many different modalities. She travels seeing clients for healing, spiritual readings, teaching healing and spiritual development.*

You may find her on the internet at jennshepherd.com

Made in the USA
Charleston, SC
01 October 2014